The *Painted* Kitchen

*Over 60 quick and easy ways
to transform your kitchen cupboards*

HENNY DONOVAN

FIREFLY BOOKS

A FIREFLY BOOK

Published by Firefly Books Ltd. 2000

First Printing

Canadian Cataloguing in Publication Data

Donovan, Henny
The painted kitchen: over 60 quick and easy ways to transform your kitchen cupboards

Includes index.
ISBN 1-55209-455-3 (bound)
ISBN 1-55209-501-0 (pbk.)

1. Kitchens. 2. Furniture painting-Amateurs' manuals. 3. Decoration and ornament. 4. Color in interior decoration. I. Title

TX653.D66 2000   643'.3   C99-931651-6

U.S. Cataloging-in-Publication Data

Donovan, Henny
The painted kitchen: over 60 quick and easy ways to transform your kitchen cupboards/ Henny Donovan. - 1st ed.
[128] p. : col. III. ; cm.
Includes index.
ISBN 1-55209-455-3 (bound)   ISBN 1-55209-501-0 (pbk.)
1. Kitchens - Remodeling. 2. Kitchens - Planning. 3. House painting. I. Title.
643/ .3 -dc 21   2000   CIP

Published in Canada in 2000 by
Firefly Books Ltd.
3680 Victoria Park Avenue
Willowdale, Ontario M2H 3K1

Published in the United States in 2000 by
Firefly Books (U.S.) Inc.
P.O. Box 1338, Ellicott Station
Buffalo, New York 14205

QUAR.TPK

Conceived, designed and produced by
Quarto Publishing plc
The Old Brewery
6 Blundell Street
London N7 9BH

Editor Steffanie Diamond Brown
Art Editor Sally Bond
Assistant Art Director Penny Cobb
Copy Editor Claire Waite
Designer Julie Francis
Photographer Paul Forrester
Picture research: Laurent Boubounelle, Frank Crawford
Indexer Dorothy Frame

Art Director Moira Clinch
Publisher Piers Spence

Manufactured in Hong Kong by Regent Publishing Services Ltd.
Printed in Singapore by Star Standard Industries (Pte) Ltd.

Contents

▲ *The pairing of silver and white in a kitchen setting creates a clean, simple, contemporary look.*

Introduction

The kitchen is increasingly becoming the heart of the home. No longer just a functional space where the task of cooking is performed, more and more people are treating the kitchen as a place to spend quality time with their families and friends. Because of this new status within the home, it is more important than ever before that the kitchen be decorated to suit the tastes and style of those who will use it most. This book was written for precisely this purpose: to help you create your ideal kitchen. Whether you want to give your existing kitchen a facelift, design a kitchen from scratch, or just disguise an unsightly feature, this book will help you create the look, feel, and ambience of the kitchen you've always dreamed of.

Paint is a simple and inexpensive way to produce a totally individual, customized look. From traditional to country, decorative to stylish, and contemporary to simple, virtually any effect you desire can be achieved with a little bit of paint and the right tools. Given the modern materials available today, the versatility of paint, and the knowledge of how to use both to produce beautiful effects, a little time and effort is all you need to achieve exactly the style and finish you want.

This book was also written in response to the ever-increasing demand for paint effects that use water-based paints, glazes and varnishes. Water-based paints and glazes are preferable to oil-based ones for many reasons: they are safer to use, easier to clean up, emit fewer odors, and are faster-drying. Further, they do not yellow, offer strength and durability, and do not pollute the atmosphere with noxious chemicals.

The first section of the book concentrates on methods of preparation and finishing, and provides guidance on choosing colors. Before you get started on any of the projects, we show you how to determine what material your doors are made from, and then how to prepare them for the fabulous paint effects to follow. The tools, brushes and basic equipment you will need to create the featured paint effects are also detailed. Because it is important to understand the uses and properties of paints, varnishes, and mediums, we have included a chart which provides this information, as well as coverage calculations to help you plan how much paint you will need. There is also a section on how to determine which paint effects can be applied to your particular cupboard doors (given the material they are made from) as well as which ones will most flatter their shape and style. A step-by-step guide to some of the most basic paint techniques—colorwashing, distressing, and various glazing effects—is also provided. Information on how to add paneling to flat doors is included as well, along with a guide to painting door hardware and restoring original pieces. Finally, we show you how to protect your painted doors so they will stay looking beautiful for a long time.

Color can be a baffling science, and so an introduction to the nature of color and its use in the context of interior decoration is provided. The basics of color theory are covered, from tone and intensity to opposite and complementary color combinations, so you can mix your own colors knowledgeably and successfully. The difference between warm and cool colors and their impact on color schemes and mood is also explained, to help you plan the right color palette to achieve the effect you want.

Organized by color, the second section of the book consists of 16 projects designed to teach you how to create some of the most stunning paint effects available today. Subtle relief stenciled effects, innovations on traditional decoupage, polished plaster finishes, contemporary decorative scripts, vinegar glazing, modern wood grain effects, and metallic finishes are only a few of the wonderful techniques covered. Simple step-by-step instructions—accompanied by color photographs of virtually each step—show you how to achieve each effect with ease.

For additional inspiration, photographs of alternative cupboard door designs are integrated throughout the

▲ *The soft bloom of a limed finish adds a sense of classic distinction to open-grained hardwood doors.*

chapters. Each photograph is accompanied by a simple explanation of how to imitate the design, cross-referencing the techniques taught within the book, so you can learn how to create these gorgeous designs yourself.

A hands-on introduction to the world of paint effects, this book will teach you how to create your own individual look, both simply and economically. With a little practice under your belt and the techniques and ideas in this book as your guide, you will be amazed at how easy it is to transform the busiest room in the house into a place you will love spending time in.

◀ *Traditional cupboard doors can be transformed into chic, stylish kitchen furnishings with this woven denim effect.*

Preparation & finishing techniques

PROFESSIONAL PAINTERS AND DECORATORS know that preparation accounts for 80 percent of the success of any decorating project. This is no less true when working on a feature as prominently visible as kitchen cupboards. Without thorough preparation, the decorative finish may not bond to the surface and can lift, peel, or scratch. Similarly, decorative finishes must be sealed and protected to withstand the wear and tear of the kitchen environment, which includes heavy use, regular cleaning, and frequent changes in heat and humidity. Plan sufficient drying time for priming and base coating, and for sealing and varnishing. The more time left between coats, the more durable the decorated surface will be.

Preparation

The preparation of your doors will be determined by their surface and the finish already on them. Ideal surfaces for painting are bare and untreated, but in many cases you will have to deal with existing paint, stains, varnish, wax or polish, or manufactured surfaces such as melamine or vinyl. Decide whether the doors need to be stripped back to their original surface, or require just simple sanding for a smooth finish. Check that the quality of the doors warrants the work, and that they can withstand the different treatments: doors that are either rickety, warped, or coming apart at the joins are not good subjects for decorative finishes, unless the finish is intended as a temporary facelift until new doors can be fitted.

The method of preparation required will also depend on the finish already on the doors. If you are unsure whether they were finished with an acrylic or oil-based product, treat them as if finished with an oil-based product. Finally, it will be easier to work on your doors if you remove them from their cupboards first.

DOOR COMPOSITION

WOOD
Solid wood: Solid wooden doors are most commonly made from pine or oak, but can also be made from mahogany, ash, maple, or birch.

Laminate: Laminate doors consist of layers of compressed wood compounds such as fiberboard or chipboard sandwiched between layers of wood such as pine, mahogany, or birch.

Veneer: Veneer is similar to laminate, but the thin layer of wood is generally stuck to a solid wood base of lesser quality.

FIBERBOARD
Made of compressed wood fibers, these doors are manufactured primarily for flat-color painting, but are perfectly suitable for many other paint finishes as well.

PLASTIC
Most man-made doors consist of some sort of plastic coating attached to a chipboard or fiberboard base. Melamine and vinyl are the most common types of plastic used, and are produced either plain or patterned, to emulate wood grains.

PREPARATION REQUIREMENTS

Surface	Method of preparation	Materials and tools
NEW, BARE WOOD *(solid wood or laminate)*	Sand and apply knot sealer. Apply two coats of acrylic primer.	Medium- and fine-grade sandpaper; varnish brush; knot sealer; natural bristle paintbrush; acrylic primer
WATER-BASED PAINTS ON WOOD *(solid wood or laminate)*	Clean, sand, and prime with acrylic primer. Where many layers of paint have been built up, use a commercial paint stripper. Sand and prime after stripping.	Diluted detergent; cloth; medium- and fine-grade sandpaper; natural bristle paintbrush; acrylic primer; gloves, goggles; paintbrush; commercial paint stripper; paint scraper
OIL-BASED PAINTS ON WOOD *(solid wood or laminate)*	Clean. Scrape off or strip uneven, flaking, or blistered paint. Sand down and fill any cracks with wood filler. Sand well and prime with acrylic primer or acrylic converter.	Diluted detergent; cloth; metal paint scraper; gloves, goggles; old paintbrush; commercial paint stripper, coarse- and medium-grade sandpaper; putty knife; wood filler; natural bristle paintbrush; acrylic primer or acrylic converter
WATER-BASED STAINS ON WOOD *(solid wood or laminate)*	Clean, sand, and prime with acrylic primer.	Diluted detergent; cloth; medium- and fine-grade sandpaper; natural bristle paintbrush; acrylic primer
OIL-BASED STAINS ON WOOD *(solid wood or laminate)*	Remove stain with steel wool and mineral spirits. Clean, sand, and prime with acrylic primer or acrylic converter.	Medium-grade steel wool; mineral spirits; medium- and fine-grade sandpaper; natural bristle paintbrush; acrylic primer or acrylic converter
WATER-BASED VARNISH ON WOOD *(solid wood or laminate)*	Clean, sand, and prime with acrylic primer.	Diluted detergent; cloth; medium- and fine-grade sandpaper; natural bristle paintbrush; acrylic primer
OIL-BASED VARNISH ON WOOD *(solid wood or laminate)*	Clean. Scrape off or strip uneven, flaking, or blistered paintwork. Sand and fill any cracks with wood filler. Sand and prime with acrylic primer or acrylic converter.	Diluted detergent; cloth; paint scraper; gloves, goggles; old paintbrush; commercial paint stripper; coarse- and medium-grade sandpaper; putty knife; wood filler; natural bristle paintbrush; acrylic primer or acrylic converter
CELLULOSE VARNISH ON WOOD *(solid wood or laminate)*	Sand with wet-dry sandpaper until smooth. Seal with white shellac and prime with acrylic primer.	Coarse- and medium-grade wet-dry sandpaper; varnish brush; white shellac; natural bristle paintbrush; acrylic primer
SHELLAC/LACQUER/ FRENCH POLISH ON WOOD *(solid wood or laminate)*	Remove polish with methylated spirits and steel wool, then neutralize with hot water and detergent. Sand and prime with acrylic primer.	Medium-grade steel wool; methylated spirits; detergent; cloth; medium-grade sandpaper; natural bristle paintbrush; acrylic primer
WAX ON WOOD *(solid wood or laminate)*	Remove wax with methylated spirits and steel wool, then neutralize with hot water and detergent. Sand, then prime with acrylic primer.	Medium-grade steel wool; methylated spirits; detergent; cloth; medium-grade sandpaper; natural bristle paintbrush; acrylic primer
WOOD VENEER	Veneer should be fully secured, not peeling or torn. Sand carefully and prime with acrylic primer.	Fine-grade sandpaper; natural bristle paintbrush; acrylic primer
BARE, NEW FIBERBOARD	Sand, then coat with watered-down white glue (1 part glue to 3 parts water). Apply acrylic primer. Make sure all edges are sealed.	Medium- and fine-grade sandpaper; two natural bristle paintbrushes; white glue; acrylic primer
WATER-BASED PAINTS ON FIBERBOARD	Clean, sand, and prime with acrylic primer.	Diluted detergent; cloth; medium- and fine-grade sandpaper; natural bristle paintbrush; acrylic primer
OIL-BASED PAINTS ON FIBERBOARD	Clean, sand, and prime with acrylic primer or acrylic converter.	Diluted detergent; cloth; coarse- and medium-grade sandpaper; natural bristle paintbrush; acrylic primer or acrylic converter
MELAMINE, FORMICA, AND VINYL	Clean with hot water and detergent. Sand with wet-dry sandpaper, then apply two coats of acrylic melamine primer or acrylic converter. Do not sand between coats.	Detergent; cloth; medium-grade wet-dry sandpaper; synthetic paintbrush; acrylic melamine primer or acrylic converter
WATER- OR OIL-BASED PAINTS ON MELAMINE, FORMICA, OR VINYL	Apply commercial paint stripper and scrape off paint. Clean with detergent, sand with wet-dry sandpaper, and prime with acrylic melamine primer or acrylic converter. Chipped, flaking surfaces are unsuitable for repainting.	Protective gloves and goggles; old paintbrush; commercial paint stripper; metal paint scraper; diluted detergent; cloth; medium-grade wet-dry sandpaper; synthetic paintbrush; acrylic melamine primer or acrylic converter

Preparation techniques

Planning enough time for preparation is just as important as allowing time for your chosen decorative technique. Although the preparation stage can be less than exciting, it is essential that it be done properly. Every moment spent preparing your doors will reap huge rewards in the long run, while skimping on this process can diminish the results—or even lead to having to redo the work.

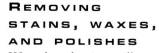

CLEANING

Ensure that any surface is clean and free of grease and loose particles. Use household detergent diluted in water or a solution of trisodium phosphate (TSP) (follow package instructions) and wipe down with a clean cloth. Avoid saturating the surface. Doors covered with thick grime will need the stronger solutions of TSP or sugar soap, both of which must be washed off after use.

STRIPPING

Layers of thick, uneven paint and varnish cannot be rubbed back with sandpaper alone; a commercial paint stripper is needed. Strip cupboard doors by hand, since professional dipping may cause warping or force the joins to come undone (and is also very costly). Wear protective gloves and goggles and follow the manufacturer's instructions. Strippers are most effective when they are applied liberally and left to soak for at least 30 minutes. Remove paint using a metal paint scraper.

REMOVING STAINS, WAXES, AND POLISHES

Water-based paints will not adhere to surfaces that have previously been stained with oil-based stains, or waxed or polished. Remove oil-based stains using medium-grade steel wool and mineral spirits; waxes, polishes, and shellacs can be removed using medium-grade steel wool and methylated spirits. Wipe down with diluted detergent or TSP. When dry, sand thoroughly.

SANDING

Sanding has many uses: it removes old paint, loose materials, and varnishes; creates a smooth working surface and a key; smooths surfaces after stripping or steel wool treatments; and smooths wooden doors between coats of primer, latex paint, and varnish. Choose coarse, medium, or fine grades in either glass or wet-dry sandpaper, depending on the smoothness required (see page 7). Sand wood in the direction of the grain; fiberboard, melamine, and vinyl should be sanded straight up and down. Wear a face mask to avoid dust inhalation.

FILLING AND SEALING WOOD

Using a putty knife, apply commercial wood filler to wooden doors with sections of grain missing or cracks in the molding. Allow to dry, then sand. Do not use resin-based fillers if you are using an acrylic primer. For paint finishes that require a smooth surface, doors with a very open grain will also need filling—fine commercial filler designed for walls can be used for this purpose. Seal knots on new, bare wooden doors by applying knot sealer with a paintbrush. This will prevent resin from the knots seeping through to the final paint finish.

PRIMING

When the surface is smooth, apply a coat of primer (see page 7 for primer type). If the base coat to follow is a strong color, tint the primer with a universal tinter for easier coverage. Primers seal the surface, provide initial coverage, and create a bond between the surface and the paint. For paneled doors, apply primer to the inner panel first, starting with the molding. Then apply liberally to the outer panel using a crisscross motion; lay off by brushing up and down. Prime the door frame following the grain's direction; apply primer first to the top and bottom, then to the vertical sides. For flat doors, apply primer liberally using a crisscross motion; lay off by brushing up and down.

APPLYING THE BASE COAT

Once the door has been primed, apply one or two coats of base color—either water-based highly pigmented wood paint or latex paint—using a household paintbrush. Apply the paint in the same way as priming, brushing it on in a crisscross motion and laying off by brushing up and down for a smooth finish. On wooden doors, sand between coats with fine-grade sandpaper. Do not sand between coats on melamine, man-made laminates, or vinyl surfaces; apply the paint on these surfaces as evenly as possible.

Paints, brushes & useful equipment

Before beginning your project, determine which equipment and materials you will need to produce the paint effect. It is important to have everything on hand, as some finishes will require you to work quickly.

USEFUL EQUIPMENT

You will find much of the general equipment used to produce paint effects around your home or in your toolbox. Other items may warrant a trip to the hardware store.

Dust sheets protect the surrounding areas from paint or solvent spills.

A **dust mask** is useful when sanding, as the fine dust produced can irritate your nose and mouth.

Sandpaper comes in a variety of grades: fine, medium, and coarse, as well as wet-dry.

Steel wool is available in different grades: fine, medium, and coarse.

A **firm wire brush** is used to rake out the grain of wood before liming.

A small, **soft wire brush** is used to remove liming paste.

Use a **decorators' sponge** (latex) to wipe down surfaces and to apply colorwash.

General-purpose **cotton cloths** are used to clean the surface in preparation, as well as for glazing techniques such as rag-rolling.

Protective gloves should be worn when using paint strippers. You may also wish to wear them when working with paints and glazes if your skin is easily irritated.

A **paint pail** is necessary for mixing paints and glazes.

A **mini roller** is used for inking up stamps.

Use a **mixing palette**, such as a plastic tub, an old plate, or a clean foil container, for mixing small amounts of paint.

Candle wax from a plain white household candle is used to create a wax resist in distressing techniques.

Low-tack spray adhesive can be used to temporarily stick stencils and other designs to surfaces.

Low-tack painters' tape is used to mask off areas you do not wish to paint.

Use **low-tack lining tape** to mask off areas when painting straight lines.

Teaspoons (tsp) and **tablespoons (tbsp)** are used when measuring out paints, glazes, and plaster.

Rags and **lint-free polishing cloths** are used to apply and buff waxes.

A **spirit level** helps mark an accurate horizontal line, and is useful when working on doors that are still attached to cupboards.

Use a **tape measure** when planning measurements over a large area.

Firm wire brush

Dust mask

Steel wool

Soft wire brush

Paint pail

Mini roller

Spoon

Mixing palette

Low-tack spray adhesive

Sandpaper

Decorators' sponge

Protective gloves

Cotton cloths

Dust sheets

Candle wax

Plastic & metal rulers, pencils, plastic eraser, transfer & tracing paper

Use an 18 or 12 in (45 or 30cm) **plastic ruler** for marking up guidelines.
A 12 in (30cm) **metal ruler** is helpful when scoring designs into wood using a craft knife.
Use a sharp **craft knife** to cut stencil designs and score into wood.
It helps to have good-quality, sharp **scissors** when cutting out decoupage motifs and metal transfer leaf.
Have a variety of **pencils** on hand for marking up guidelines and designs.
A **plastic** or **gum eraser** will remove pencil marks once a decoration has dried.
Transfer paper and **tracing paper** are used to transfer drawn or photocopied designs onto a surface.
Have photocopy, laser, or layout paper on hand for sketches, designs, and layouts, and for keeping track of measurements.

Lint-free cloth

Craft knife

Tape measure

Scissors

Spirit level

ow-tack painters' r lining tape

PAINTS, VARNISHES, AND SPECIALIST MEDIUMS

Paint is made up of three main ingredients: pigment, binder, and a medium or vehicle. The pigment provides color and covering power; the binder, which hardens as it dries, causes adhesion to the surface, and the medium makes application possible. There are three main paint families: water-based, oil-based, and alcohol-based. Solvents are used to dissolve the paint and make cleaning possible. The solvent for water-based paint is water; for oil-based paint use mineral spirits or turpentine, and for alcohol-based paint use methylated spirits. Most of the products used in this book are water-based, with the exception of shellac, wax, and polyurethane varnish. Water-based products are preferable in that they are easy to use, non-toxic, virtually odorless, and environmentally safe (they must be disposed of in accordance with local waste regulations, however). This chart highlights some of the products available for painting, staining, varnishing, waxing, and creating special effects.

Product	Water-based varieties	Oil-based varieties	Alcohol-based varieties
PRIMERS AND DECORATING PAINTS FOR FURNITURE AND WOODWORK	Acrylic primer Acrylic converter Melamine primer Latex paint High pigment paint (undiluted) Stencil paint	Oil undercoat Semi-gloss paint Gloss paint Enamel/Japan paint	Cellulose paint
ARTISTS' PAINTS FOR APPLIED DECORATION AND TINTING	Artists' acrylic paint Gouache Universal tinter	Artists' oil paint Oil pastel	
SPECIALIST EFFECTS AND FINISHES	Acrylic glazing liquid Colorwash Impasto, polished plaster Combing paste Liming paste Crackle glaze Craquelure varnish	Oil-based glazing liquid Linseed oil	White shellac Button polish shellac Amber or orange shellac
BINDERS FOR SPECIALIST FINISHES	White glue Rabbit-skin glue Acrylic gilding size	Japan gilding size	
STAINS	Highly pigmented wood paint (diluted) Water-based stains and dyes Universal tinter	Oil-based stains	
WAXES		Colored wax Beeswax Paraffin wax Carnauba wax Liming wax	
VARNISHES AND SEALERS	Matte acrylic varnish Semi-gloss acrylic varnish Gloss acrylic varnish Metallic acrylic varnish	Flat oil-based varnish Semi-gloss oil-based varnish Gloss oil-based varnish Polyurethane varnish Marine varnish	Knot sealer Shellac

BRUSHES AND THEIR USES

Brush	Used for	Technique
1 AND 2 IN (25 AND 50MM) NATURAL BRISTLE PAINTBRUSHES	Priming, applying latex paint and wood paint, and general usage.	Load a liberal amount of paint onto the tip of the brush. Paint using crisscross strokes followed by straight strokes.
1 AND 2 IN (25 AND 50MM) SYNTHETIC PAINTBRUSHES	Priming and painting onto man-made surfaces; good for most acrylic paints.	Load a liberal amount of paint onto the tip of the brush. Paint using crisscross strokes followed by straight strokes.
1 AND 2 IN (25 AND 50MM) VARNISH BRUSHES	Applying varnishes and shellacs.	Do not overload the brush. Glide the brush over the surface using light, smooth strokes.
FITCH BRUSH	Mixing paints, painting panels and moldings, and painting small areas and edges.	Use the tip of the brush to work the paint.
ARTISTS' SABLE BRUSH	Hand-painting and detail, and applying gilding size to small areas.	Keep the paint on the tip of the brush for optimum control. For loose strokes, as in a folk art style, hold the brush in the middle of the handle. For more controlled work, hold the brush nearer to the base of the bristles.
$\frac{1}{4}$ AND $\frac{1}{2}$ IN (6 AND 13MM) SABLE OR NYLON ONE-STROKE BRUSHES	Hand-painting, applying washes to small areas and moldings; good for creating clean edges.	For washes, hold the brush in the middle of the handle and load liberally with paint. For more detailed work, hold the handle nearer to the base of the bristles and use less paint.
STENCIL BRUSH	Stenciling, stippling; good for fine spattering.	When stenciling, always choose a large brush. Control the brush by placing an elastic band around the base of the bristles. Always use a dry brush and as little paint as possible when stenciling.
HOG-HAIR SOFTENER	Softening and blending colorwash effects (apply colorwash with decorators' sponge first); can also be used for stippling, and for moving glaze as it becomes sticky.	Hold the brush handle nearer to the base of the bristles and use soft, long, sweeping crisscross movements.
STIPPLING BLOCK	Stippling glazing liquid and textured effects in thick paint.	Used in a "pouncing" motion, either for its own effect or for evening out glaze before dragging or combing. Dab the block at right angles to the surface.
DRAGGING BRUSH	Dragging through glazing liquid.	Drag the brush down through the glaze, or toward you if working flat. Repeat this action in downward stripes until complete. Some areas may need going over again for an even dragged effect.
FLOGGING BRUSH	Wood graining and some marble effects; can also be used for dragging.	Starting at the bottom of the glazed area, hit the surface in a flogging action with the flat tip of the brush moving upward, or away from you if working flat. Repeat from bottom to top until complete.
PENCIL OVERGRAINER	Wood graining and some marble finishes.	Pull the overgrainer down through the glaze in a swerving motion—the degree of waviness will depend on the desired grain effect.
BADGER-HAIR SOFTENER	Wood graining and marbling; used to soften the marks created by a previous brush.	Lightly brush over the marks already made in the same and opposite directions.
RUBBER COMBING TOOL	Combing glazing liquid and textured paints.	For straight lines, comb toward you or downward. For wavy lines or other effects, comb freestyle.
DECORATORS' STEEL FLOAT	Application and smoothing of polished plaster work such as Venetian plaster, marmorino, and stucco.	Take up some plaster onto the float and smooth over the surface in an arcing movement. Repeat action to remove any excess plaster and ridges.

Natural bristle paintbrush

Synthetic paintbrush

Varnish brush

Small decorators' brush

Fitch brush

Stencil brush

Artists' sable brushes

Hog-hair softener

Stippling block

Pencil overgrainer

Badger-hair softener

Flogging brush

Dragging brush

Rubber combing tool

Decorators' steel float

CARE OF BRUSHES

- Brushes are an expensive investment, but will last for a long time if properly cared for. Do not soak brushes for long periods, as this loosens the glue that holds the bristles in place. Wash brushes immediately after use to avoid paint caking in the bristles. For water-based paints and varnishes, remove excess paint with water, then put some detergent onto the bristles and work through with a nail or dishwashing brush to remove all traces of paint. Rinse, then dip in fabric softener or hair conditioner to condition the bristles. Rinse again, then squeeze out. Shake off excess water and leave to dry—flat initially and then hanging, if possible. For oil-based paints and varnishes, rinse first with white spirit, then clean with detergent, rinse with water, condition, and leave to dry, as above. For alcohol-based products, remove all traces of the product by dousing the brush in methylated spirits. Clean with detergent, then rinse with water, condition, and leave to dry, as above. Never leave shellac on a brush; once it hardens, it is impossible to remove.

- Always wash a badger-hair softener immediately after use, as dry paint cannot be removed from the brush and will greatly reduce its softening ability. The brush can be dried using a hair dryer.

UNIVERSAL TINTER GUIDELINES

Universal tinters or stainers are highly concentrated coloring agents. Care should always be taken when using them, especially as some colors are stronger than others. The strength of the color obtained will depend upon the medium being tinted and the amount of white within that medium. It is important to note that tinters have no binder and no drying power of their own, so if you wish to use them for hand-painting, they must be mixed with a medium that has a built-in binder, such as a varnish, glazing liquid, or artists' acrylics. The following chart is offered as a guideline for strength and usage, and roughly reflects the amount of medium that can be used for two doors. As a general rule, add the tinter a drop or two at a time, monitoring the results as you go. Amounts will vary between brands, so always check the manufacturer's instructions before use, and test for varying strengths.

Color	Medium	Pastel shade	Mid-tone	Full color	Medium	Pastel shade	Mid-tone	Full color
RAW UMBER, BURNT UMBER	Glazing liquid	2 drops	5 drops	10-15 drops	White latex paint and polished plaster	5-10 drops	20-30 drops	50-60 drops
RED IRON OXIDE, RED, BURNT SIENNA	Glazing liquid	1 drop	3 drops	6-8 drops	White latex paint and polished plaster	3 drops	6-8 drops	15-20 drops
YELLOW OCHER, YELLOW	Glazing liquid	3 drops	6-8 drops	15-20 drops	White latex paint and polished plaster	10 drops	30 drops	50-60 drops
GREEN, BLUE, PURPLE	Glazing liquid	2 drops	5 drops	10-15 drops	White latex paint and polished plaster	5-10 drops	20-30 drops	50-60 drops
WHITE	Glazing liquid	2 drops	5 drops	10-15 drops	White latex paint and polished plaster	10 drops	30 drops	60 drops

HEALTH AND SAFETY

- *Be sure to read and follow the manufacturer's instructions carefully on all products.*

- *Always work in a well-ventilated area.*

- *Wear protective rubber gloves to avoid direct skin contact when using oil- and alcohol-based products.*

- *When using water-based products, avoid lengthy exposure to the skin, as this can cause the skin to dry out. Wear protective gloves if you have sensitive skin.*

WHAT DO THE PRODUCTS DO?

This chart provides a brief description of the main paints and materials used in this book and explains what they are used for. There is also a coverage calculation reference, to help you plan how much of each product you will need.

Paints and materials	Product description	Paints and materials	Product description
ACRYLIC PRIMER Coverage: 1L up to 12m² (1 qt up to 108 ft²)	A water-based primer for sealing and covering wood and fiberboard surfaces.	**UNIVERSAL TINTERS** Coverage: see tinter chart, left	Versatile, water-based tinting agent. Highly concentrated liquid color that disperses well in all products. Can also be used to color thick textured paints, plaster finishes, limewash, distemper, acrylic varnish, shellac, and oil-based paints. Not suitable for use with cellulose-based mediums.
MELAMINE PRIMER OR ACRYLIC CONVERTER Coverage: 1L up to 12m² (1 qt up to 108 ft²)	A water-based primer for sealing and covering melamine, vinyl, and other man-made surfaces. Can also be painted over oil-based paints (after sanding) as a base for water-based paints.	**IMPASTO** Coverage: 1L up to 4m² (1 qt up to 36 ft²)	Thick paint designed for textured effects on walls, but equally effective on furniture as a relief-stenciling medium. Can be colored with universal tinters, or colorwashed.
LATEX PAINT Coverage: 1L up to 10m² (1 qt up to 90 ft²)	A water-based paint designed for use on walls, but can be used for most furniture as well. Available in matte (flat) and satin (mid-sheen) finishes.	**POLISHED PLASTER/VENETIAN PLASTER/MARMORINO** Coverage: 1kg up to 1m² (3 lb up to 10 ft²)	Specialist plaster finish for distressed and polished effects. The plaster contains lime and marble dust, and can be polished with a decorators' float for a smooth finish. Color with universal tinters or dry pigments (need to be dissolved first). Beautiful when colorwashed.
WOOD PAINT Coverage: 1L undiluted up to 12m² (1 qt up to 108 ft²)	A matte, opaque, undiluted paint specially formulated for wood. Contains a built-in primer, and has a high chalk and pigment content. It covers well and is of better quality than latex paint. Ideal for high-quality flat-color painting, distressing, burnishing, and stenciling. Can also be diluted with water to create a wash for bare wood. Should not be confused with colorwash.	**LIMING PASTE** Coverage: 1L up to 16m² (1 qt up to 144 ft²)	Thick, chalky, water-based paste applied to hardwoods with an open grain. Remove with a soft wire brush once dry for a silvery bloom. Seal with white shellac and acrylic varnish.
STENCIL PAINT Approximate coverage: 4.5L up to 500m² (4.5 qt up to 4500 ft²)	Specialist water-based paint formulated for stenciling and stamping. Good for hand-painting.	**CRACKLE GLAZE** Coverage: 1L up to 16m² (1 qt up to 144 ft²)	When applied between two layers of water-based paint, this water-based medium causes the top coat of paint to crack and open up, revealing the color underneath.
ARTISTS' ACRYLIC PAINT Coverage: A good squeeze will tint 500ml (½ qt) by one shade	Good for hand-painting. They can also be used for tinting glazes or paints, but must be diluted first to guarantee proper color dispersion. Not as strong or cheap as universal tinters, but possess good adhesive properties.	**CRAQUELURE VARNISH** Coverage: 1L up to 16m² (1 qt up to 144 ft²)	A water-based, two-step cracking varnish that produces an antiqued effect over painted surfaces and decoupage. The top coat varnish is applied over the dry base coat varnish. As the top coat dries, cracks appear due to a reaction between the two layers. Artists' oil paint or colored wax is rubbed into the cracks for emphasis.
GLAZING LIQUID (ACRYLIC) Coverage: 1L up to 16m² (1 qt up to 144 ft²), although varies according to dilution	Water-based, transparent, colorless glaze. Tint to required color with universal tinters or artists' acrylic paints. Used for many paint effects, including combing, stippling, wood graining and marbling. A drying retardant such as glycol may be added to slow drying time. Dries to a satin finish. Seal and protect with acrylic varnish.	**ACRYLIC GILDING SIZE** Approximate Coverage: 60ml up to 1m² (1 qt up to 300 ft²)	Water-based glue used to adhere metal leaf and metallic powders.
COLORWASH Coverage: 1L up to 30m² (1 qt up to 270 ft²)	Specially formulated, water-based, translucent, colored glaze containing glycol retardants. Also available clear for tinting. If not available ready-made, can be created by mixing three parts liquid glaze (preferably matte) with one part water to the consistency of light cream. Can be tinted using universal tinter. Creates a soft bloom of color with a matte finish.	**ACRYLIC VARNISH** Coverage: 1L up to 16m² (1 qt up to 144 ft²)	Water-based varnish available in matte, semi-gloss, or gloss finishes. Quick-drying.
		SHELLAC Approximate coverage: 1L up to 8m² (1 qt up to 72ft²)	Alcohol-based, fast-drying lacquer. White and button polish shellacs are used to seal many decorative finishes. Enables the transfer of work between oil- and water-based mediums. Does not replace varnish, and requires a protective coat.

Door types

Kitchen cupboard doors are made from a variety of materials with a range of finishes. A basic ability to identify which material a door is made from is necessary in order to ascertain its suitability for a particular paint finish.

The materials from which kitchen cupboard doors are made typically fall into two categories: wooden and man-made. Both categories of materials appear in many forms, however, and it can thus be difficult to tell the two types apart: solid woods can resemble laminates, and man-made materials often imitate woods. An examination of the door's joints may help reveal its true nature: wooden doors, unless they are a single carved piece, have genuine joints, such as "dovetailed" joints, clearly visible at the top and bottom edges; all laminates, whether natural or plastic, have visible (if only faintly) seams on their inside edges; and man-made doors that emulate wood usually have no joints at all.

The categories "wooden" and "man-made" can be broken down even further. Wooden cupboard doors can be made from solid wood, laminate, or veneer; fiberboard doors are made from compressed wood fibers; and plastic doors are typically made from melamine or vinyl attached to a fiberboard base (see page 6 for further detail).

▼ *Featured from far left to right*: Solid oak door, made from bare, untreated wood; solid pine door, made from untreated, knotty pine; melamine affixed to a fiberboard base; cherry wood vinyl wrapped onto a shaped chipboard base.

SUITABILITY OF SURFACES

Wooden surfaces are almost always the most suitable base for paint finishes. This is because paint bonds well to wood, thereby increasing the life span of the finish and enhancing its beauty. Paint finishes on wooden surfaces are also less prone to cracking and chipping. Finishes suitable for wooden surfaces include flat-color painting, distressing, liming, faux marquetry, leaf stippling, impasto relief stenciling, combing, vinegar glaze effects, liquid glaze effects, craquelure, crackle glaze, stenciling, stamping, and hand-painting. Polished plaster and stucco effects work best on fiberboard surfaces.

Good results can be obtained on melamine and vinyl surfaces as well, as long as plenty of drying time is allowed (for each layer to fully cure and bond). The application of a paint finish to a plastic surface is recommended as a temporary measure only; it is not a long-term solution. The paint effects that work best on melamine and vinyl surfaces are those that do not involve thickly textured paints and plasters, and do not require the type of vigorous working which might cause the underlying coats of paint to peel away. Suitable finishes for use on these surfaces include flat-color painting, colorwashing, dry-brush work, stenciling, stamping, hand-painting, decoupage, checks, and wood graining (the latter two effects will need extra drying time).

Countertops and work surfaces should not be embellished with paint effects, since they receive too much wear and tear. A very simple effect, such as stenciling or stamping, could be added to solid wooden worktops, but only if protected with several coats of marine varnish.

Do not attempt extensive paint treatments on doors that are chipped, or on doors where the laminate is coming away from the base, as the paint may bubble and scratch and will not last.

Matching door styles
with paint effects

There are many different styles of kitchen cupboard doors: flat, tongue-and-groove, Shaker-style, classic paneled country-style, modern with a small inner panel and a wide frame, and traditional with a raised central panel and an arched top are some well-known examples. Contemporary door styles tend to show simple lines and very little detail, while many traditional doors have detailed paneling and frames. While most paint finishes are versatile enough to be adapted to suit a multitude of different door styles, certain finishes are better suited to some styles than others. As a general rule, flat doors or doors with wide

Shaker-style frames are best for more modern, contemporary designs, such as those achieved using polished plaster or metallic paints. Doors with molding or paneling are very well-suited to more traditional paint effects, such as distressing; they also work well in conjunction with elaborate finishes, notably those in which hand-painted detail covers only a section of the door. An example of each type of finish—modern, traditional, and elaborate—is shown below, having been applied to the particular door style that flatters it most.

▲ Polished plaster finishes work especially well on plain, flat surfaces, such as this fiberboard door. The flatness of the surface makes the application of the plaster easier, and complements the modern look created by this technique.

▲ Paneled or tongue-and-grooved doors are well-suited to distressed finishes, for which the molding or detail acts as the worn edge. Here the distressing is light enough so as not to dominate the overall look, yet it is visible enough to highlight the molding and hand-painted script.

▲ A raised inner panel and molding can act as a natural frame for a hand-painted motif such as this folk art design.

Choosing a technique

When deciding on a paint effect, think about the look you're after. The color scheme and door style will both be relevant factors to consider. After choosing a paint effect and color scheme, practice the technique and try mixing the colors before painting on the actual door. Below is an overview of some of the most commonly used techniques.

DISTRESSING

Distressed paintwork has a timeless appeal. This technique requires some patience because of the many layers of paint involved, but it will last a long time. Examples of distressing can be seen on pages 34-37, 87, 102, 103, and 105. Prime the door (see pages 6-9) and apply two coats of highly pigmented wood paint or matte latex paint using crisscross movements, laid on in vertical strokes. Smooth with fine-grade sandpaper.

1 Rub a household candle onto areas most likely to wear, such as moldings and corners, and onto some flat areas. Do not cover the whole door. Go back over the same areas to ensure a build-up of wax.

2 Apply one or two coats of highly pigmented wood paint or matte latex paint (depending on the strength of the base color and the amount required for coverage) in a second color. The paint may become bumpy as it reacts with the wax. Leave to dry.

3 Use medium-grade steel wool or sandpaper to lightly rub paint back from the waxed areas, revealing the base coat beneath. If the steel wool produces gray marks, these can be removed with soapy water. Keep the distressing subtle for a realistic look. Finish by sanding over the whole door with fine-grade sandpaper to create a burnished, smooth surface. Seal with two coats of matte acrylic varnish.

COLORWASHING

In this technique, the base paint shows through the top coat to reveal soft, broken color. Examples of colorwashing can be seen on pages 43, 72-75, 85, and 104. Work on one door at a time. After priming (see pages 6-9), apply two even coats of base color using the same technique as for distressing. Use either non-absorbent matte latex paint or ordinary matte latex paint sealed with matte acrylic varnish. Leave to dry for a minimum of 24 hours, then apply the colorwash, as below. If ready-made colorwash is unavailable, mix three parts liquid glaze (preferably matte) and one part water to the consistency of light cream. Tint with universal tinter to the desired shade (see tinter guidelines, page 14), and apply as below.

1 Pour approximately 1 tbsp (15ml) of colorwash onto a decorators' sponge.

2 Wipe the colorwash onto the door surface in swirling figure-of-eight movements, until the whole door is covered. Make sure that there are no gaps in the colorwash.

3 Brush over the colorwash with a hog-hair softener immediately, using light crisscross movements to soften the effect. Work swiftly, before the colorwash becomes tacky. Allow to dry for 24 hours, then apply a coat of matte acrylic varnish. Decorate further as desired, then finish with three coats of matte acrylic varnish.

LIQUID GLAZE EFFECTS

These effects should always be applied on non-absorbent surfaces painted with either vinyl satin paint, acrylic eggshell paint, or a paint varnished with a semi-gloss acrylic varnish. Always allow 24 hours for the glaze to harden, then finish with three coats of matte or semi-gloss acrylic varnish.

Here we look at a number of liquid glaze effects that work well on cupboard doors. The same glaze is used for each effect, but the tools and techniques used to make patterns on the wet glaze differ. Examples of liquid glaze effects can be seen on pages 52-55, 121 (combing); 90-93, 105 (dragging); 44, 85, 94-97, 122 (spattering); and 45, 108-111 (rag-rolling).

1 Mix two-thirds acrylic glazing liquid with the final third made of equal parts matte acrylic varnish and water. Add a universal tinter if desired (see guidelines, page 14). Here we have used 4 drops of burnt sienna and 2 drops of raw umber tinter. Stir well. Mix a bit of matte acrylic varnish into the glaze to speed up drying time and for durability.

2 Use a 1 in (25mm) paint- or varnish brush to apply the glaze to the whole surface. Brush out the glaze in crisscross movements, then even it out using vertical strokes. You will need about 1 tbsp (15ml) of glaze for an average-sized door. After the glaze has been laid on, the desired technique can be applied. Changes will be hard to make once the glaze becomes sticky, but you can always wipe it off completely with a damp cloth and start again.

DRAGGING

Use a small dragging brush for paneled doors and a full-size brush for flat surfaces. Drag through the glaze to achieve an even pattern.

COMBING

Both rubber and steel combs with different sized teeth are available. Use either to create straight lines, checks, circles, or swirls.

STIPPLING

"Pounce" a stippling block firmly up and down onto the glaze, holding the block at a right angle to the surface, until the texture is consistent. Remove excess glaze from the block as you go.

SPONGING

Dampen a sea sponge and squeeze out any excess water. Lightly bounce the sponge over the glaze, creating a soft, mottled texture. Subtle (ie close in tone or tint) color combinations work best.

RAG-ROLLING

Dampen a lint-free cloth. Scrunch into a ball, then twist into a "sausage" shape. Start at the bottom and roll the cloth upwards in an arc. Repeat over the entire door.

SPATTERING

Dip a stencil brush into the glaze, shaking off any excess. Flick the brush down over your finger. Repeat over the entire door (be sure to protect surrounding areas).

Door hardware

Door hardware has become a fashionable interior accessory in its own right, with countless styles and finishes on the market to choose from. Junk shops are always worth a trawl for old handles or knobs that can be restored, and plain wooden knobs can be bought and painted to match or contrast with the paint effect on the door.

PLAIN WOODEN KNOBS

Virtually all of the techniques in this book can be applied to a plain wooden door knob. A few simple options designed to complement a wide range of different door decorations are illustrated here. If you decide to paint your knobs to match your doors exactly, do so at the same time as you paint your doors to avoid having to remix colors or glazes.

CRAQUELURE

Base coat the knob with an ivory matte latex or high-pigment wood paint. Shellac, then apply both steps of the craquelure varnish. When dry, rub raw umber artists' oil paint into the cracks and buff with a cloth. Allow to dry for 24 hours. Apply a coat of shellac and then matte polyurethane varnish or semi-gloss acrylic varnish.

METALLIC COATING

This medium is available through specialist artists' outlets. Apply the coating to the knob following the manufacturer's instructions, and allow to harden for 24 hours. Rub with medium-grade steel wool to reveal the sheen, then burnish with the back of a spoon to create extra shine.

COLORWASHING AND WAXING

Prime the knob (see pages 6-9) and apply a base coat, then colorwash to match the door's decoration (see Colorwashing, page 18). For further depth of color and extra sheen, try applying an antiquing or colored wax. Buff with a clean cloth.

RESTORING ORIGINAL PIECES

If your door hardware is made of brass, it may be tarnished or covered with lacquer or paint. To remove tarnish, soak in household vinegar overnight, then rub back with steel wool. Finish with a commercial brass cleaner. To remove lacquer, use a lacquer thinner, following the manufacturer's instructions. Add one part methylated spirits to four parts lacquer thinner to speed up the process. Rub back with steel wool. To remove paint, use a commercial paint stripper following the manufacturer's instructions. Use steel wool to remove any stubborn bits of paint. Always wear protective gloves and work in a well-ventilated area when using chemicals.

Turning flat doors
into paneled doors

A plain, flat door can be livened up considerably by the addition of a frame of beading or molding. These embellishments can also be useful if you wish to use a paint finish that requires raised areas on the door, such as distressed finishes, hand-painted detail that benefits from a frame, or finishes that are only applied to one section of the door, such as craquelure or crackle glazing.

A range of different kinds of beading and molding are available at good lumberyards, where you can have the pieces custom cut and mitered (diagonally cut). Give the lumberyard the inside measurements of the four lengths that comprise the rectangular frame.

3 Place the four lengths of 45-degree mitered wood on the glue. Make sure all the corners are at 90-degree angles—use a carpenters' square or triangle to check. Press down firmly.

4 Take some 1 in (25mm) tacks (smaller for beading that has less depth), and hammer them through the beading to fully secure it to the door surface. Use up to three tacks on the longer lengths and two on the shorter ones. If there are any gaps in the joints, fill using a commercial wood filler (follow the manufacturer's instructions). Leave to dry for 24 hours, then sand as necessary.

1 Using a pencil and ruler, draw a rectangle onto the door that matches the size of your beading strips. Make sure the rectangle is aligned "square" to the door.

2 Apply undiluted white glue to the marked area; alternatively, apply the glue to the back of the beading. Leave for about five minutes, or until the glue is tacky.

Finishing *techniques*

Care taken in finishing your doors is particularly important in the kitchen, which receives some of the heaviest wear and tear in a house. The doors must be carefully sealed and protected with varnish so they can be wiped down regularly and will stay looking good.

TYPES OF FINISHES

With its shiny, varnish-like finish, shellac can be used as a sealer, but it is not strong enough to be used on its own as a protector; it must be finished with varnish as well.

Water-based acrylic varnishes are easy to use as well as durable. They are also preferable because they do not discolor over time, as all oil-based varnishes do. Most of the projects in this book are finished with acrylic varnishes for this reason, with the occasional use of oil-based polyurethane varnish, where an aging, yellowing look is actually desired.

Waxes provide a water-resistant finish only; they are not waterproof, and thus are not generally suitable for the kitchen (although they are fine on overhead cupboards). Colored wax can, however, be used sparingly over a pre-varnished surface on small sections of a door, as the varnish will enable the surface to be wiped down. Water splashes will mark a waxed surface over time, so do not use wax near sink areas.

SHELLAC

Shellac is used for sealing gilded and decoupaged effects, and on paint finishes for a lacquer-style finish before varnishing. White shellac is bleached, so it won't discolor the finish it is being applied to. Button polish shellac is honey-colored, and is perfect for achieving an instant antiqued look. If button polish is unavailable, tint white polish with burnt sienna, raw umber, and yellow ocher universal tinters for a similar look. The solvent in shellac (denatured alcohol) evaporates rapidly, so careful application is required. Dip a varnish brush into the shellac and glide it onto the surface. After laying on, brush through only twice before evaporation starts, or the smooth look will be spoiled. A single coat should take 15-20 minutes to dry. Wait two hours before applying a top coat of varnish.

HEALTH AND SAFETY

- *Always read and follow the manufacturer's instructions on all products, and work in a well-ventilated area.*

- *When using oil- and alcohol-based products, wear protective rubber gloves to avoid direct skin contact.*

- *When using water-based products, avoid lengthy exposure to the skin. Wear protective gloves if your skin is sensitive.*

- *Dispose of all leftover products and soiled rags according to the manufacturer's instructions and local regulations.*

ACRYLIC VARNISH

A water-based varnish, acrylic varnish is available in matte, semi-gloss, and gloss finishes. Paint effects with a chalky, matte look, such as colorwashing, are best protected with matte varnish. Semi-gloss and gloss varnishes are better for gilding and dark colors, as these styles suit a reflective surface, and because matte varnish can result in a milky look. Using a varnish brush, apply an even coat of varnish over the surface, brushing it out to avoid ridges. The white sheen will disappear once dry. Apply a minimum of two coats.

POLYURETHANE AND URALKYD VARNISH

Polyurethane varnish is an inexpensive and easy-to-use oil-based varnish. It is available in matte, semi-gloss, and gloss finishes. With exposure to light, oxidation will occur, causing yellowing. This varnish is recoatable within six hours and has a strong, durable finish. Uralkyd varnishes contain a UV filter to combat yellowing, so they are clearer than plain polyurethane varnishes. These varnishes are also strong and durable. Using a varnish brush, apply an even coat of varnish over the surface, brushing it out thoroughly to avoid unevenness. Sand lightly with fine-grade sandpaper between coats, removing dust with a cloth slightly dampened with mineral spirits.

SPECIALIST AND METALLIC VARNISHES

Modern advances have led to the development of metallic finishes, thereby extending the range of varnishing options available. These metallic varnishes can be purchased at specialist outlets, and come in pearlescent, graphite, gold, silver, and copper finishes. They are recoatable after one hour, and are best applied over prepainted surfaces. Use a varnish brush to evenly lay on the varnish. Lay off in one direction only; the direction of the brush affects the way the varnish reflects light, so brush upward *or* downward (but not both), or you will end up with a striped effect. Work quickly, as these varnishes are quick-drying. Recoat after one hour for extra depth of color or for a stronger metallic effect.

COLORED WAX AND GILDING WAX

Both waxes are generally used to highlight moldings or paneling. They are best applied after one or two coats of acrylic varnish. Using a lint-free cloth, apply colored wax to the desired area. Wait five minutes, then buff. Using a lint-free cloth or a sable paintbush, apply gilding wax to the desired area. Leave as is, or buff. Do not use wax near sink areas.

LIQUID WAXES

Liquid waxes are available from specialist outlets and are easy to use. Use them only on doors that will not be subject to a lot of moisture or will not need repeated cleaning. Brush on the wax using a varnish brush. Leave for about 20 minutes, then buff with a lint-free cloth.

Choosing *colors*

The most important color decision for any room in the house is which color to paint the walls. The kitchen is the exception to this rule: cupboard doors are the most prominent surface space in this room, and thus their color will define its mood. The walls are also an important feature, however, and so it is important to coordinate their color scheme with that of the cupboard doors. You may decide to go for softer, broken color on the walls—a colorwash, perhaps—and a bright splash of solid color on the doors; or, conversely, you may prefer a subtle, distressed finish on the doors and simple, flat-color painted walls.

The next few pages provide all the information you will need to make the right color decisions, from color basics and mixing to using color to create a desired mood. Some important advice: give yourself plenty of planning time, get to know the unique features of your kitchen, and experiment with various color palettes by mixing up samples before making your final decision.

UNDERSTANDING COLOR BASICS

Understanding a few basics about color and the theory behind it is all you really need to get started; the rest is up to your imagination, and is all about having the confidence to experiment.

Beyond the basics, the choice of color is subjective; it is all about what works best for you. Try out different color combinations on sheets of paper and hold them up to your cupboard doors or the walls in your kitchen to help you visualize how they will look. When you find something you like, test it out by painting a small section of the door or wall; if it grabs you, go with it. Remember, if you make a mistake on the walls, the color can be changed fairly easily—it is the doors you need to be completely sure about!

PRIMARY, SECONDARY, AND TERTIARY COLORS

Primary colors are those that cannot be created by mixing together any other color; in other words, they are the colors from which all other colors derive. There are three primary colors: red, blue, and yellow. Secondary colors are made by mixing two primary colors together: yellow and blue make green, yellow and red make orange, and red and blue make purple. Tertiary colors are made by mixing primaries and secondaries together, creating a range of browns, grays, "dirty" purples, and greens—even black can be made in this way.

WARM AND COOL COLORS

All colors can be either warm or cool. It is easy to see where each color lies on the color wheel, where the predominantly warm and cool sides are apparent. It gets a bit more complicated, however, as warm and cool versions of the same color exist on either side of the spectrum. For instance, there are both warm and cool blues, reds, and yellows. This fact has implications for the mixing of paint, glaze, and tinter colors in the context of decorative painting. For instance, when a warm red such as vermilion is mixed with a warm blue such as cerulean, the result is a chocolatey brown; whereas when a cool red such as alizarin crimson is mixed with a cool blue such as ultramarine or cobalt, the result is a deep violet.

The illustrations to the right show the three primary colors in both their warm and cool incarnations. Together, these six pigments provide a comprehensive palette from which any color in the spectrum can be created.

Warm red • *Vermilion*

Cool red • *Alizarin crimson*

Warm yellow • *Cadmium yellow*

Cool yellow • *Lemon yellow*

Cool blue • *Ultramarine or Cobalt*

Warm blue • *Cerulean*

The Color Wheel

OPPOSITE OR COMPLEMENTARY COLORS

An understanding of the principle of opposite or complementary colors is important when choosing colors for a room. The opposite color of each primary color is the secondary color sitting opposite it on the color wheel. Thus, the opposite of red is green, the opposite of blue is orange, and the opposite of yellow is purple. The pairing of opposite colors in a color scheme can provide a welcome color contrast.

Mixing equal proportions of opposite colors will create a range of browns and grays; adding just a bit of the opposite color will tone down or "dirty" a color.

WHITE

White is considered to be the absence of color, as it reflects all light. In a room scheme it is highly reflective, lightening dark areas and making small areas seem larger. It also lends itself to virtually all color schemes, and can be used as part of any style of decoration. In terms of mood, off-white is easier to live with than brilliant white, which has a blue tint and thus a chilly edge.

As might be expected, white is one of the most widely used pigments, instantly adding opacity to colors (most of which have a high degree of translucency), thereby increasing its coverage ability. Adding white to a color will also instantly cool it down. Further, the more white that is added to a color, the more evident its pastel tones will become.

EARTH COLORS

Earth colors were the first pigments discovered by humankind. Literally hewn from the ground, they were mixed with water and dabbed onto the walls of early cave dwellings. Today, raw umber, burnt umber, raw sienna, burnt sienna, red iron oxide, and yellow ocher are the most common earth colors used, although a multitude of variations is available.

Earth colors have both warm and cold elements. Raw umber, for example, is the cooler version of the two umbers. Always keep some raw umber, burnt sienna, and yellow ocher on hand when mixing glazes and tinting paints, as these colors are uniquely useful for aging, "dirtying," toning down, and warming up all colors.

Raw Umber

Burnt Umber

Raw Sienna

Burnt Sienna

Red Iron Oxide

Yellow Ocher

METALLICS

Metallic pigments are made from ground metals, which account for their luster and reflective qualities. All metallic paint has a certain amount of metallic pigment in it—the more pigment, the better the quality and coverage—so expect to pay more for these paints (it is worth buying the best quality you can afford). A range of metallic varnishes and paints is now available in silvers, golds, and coppers, as well as pearlescent and graphite. These paints are not designed to mix with other colors, and are best applied in their own right, in sections or over appropriate bases. Given the translucent nature of metallic paint, be sure to choose a base color that takes into account—and will enhance—the metallic finish. For example, pearlescent metallic varnish is beautiful over cool pastel blues and greens; silver works well over cool grays; and gold looks wonderful over warm, sandy tones.

USING COLOR TO CREATE MOOD

The use of color can significantly affect the mood of a space. Certain color combinations can make a room feel cosy and friendly, while others will give it a cooler feel. The basic rules on using color to create mood are detailed below.

COLOR AND LIGHT

The amount of light in a room will affect your choice of color. In general, lighter, brighter colors reflect light, while darker colors absorb it. Bear this fact in mind when deciding whether to use dark or light colors in your color scheme, and consider it as well in relation to the size of your kitchen. Remember also that the finish—gloss or matte—will also affect the degree of light reflection or absorption.

▲ *This soft blue colorwash effect is significantly enlivened by the complementary warm orange tones of both the wicker basket and the wood revealed through the cupboard doors.*

▲ *In this kitchen setting, warm egg-yolk yellows are paired with cool, chalky greens, demonstrating how warm and cool colors can be used together for a beautiful effect.*

WARM AND COOL COLORS

The use of warm and cool colors will dramatically affect the mood of a room. Generally, warmer colors will seem to fill a space more, giving it a more closed-in feeling, whereas cooler colors will open a space up, creating a lighter, airier environment. This does not mean that warm colors should be avoided in small spaces and cool colors in large spaces; the decision depends entirely on the mood you wish to create. You may want a small kitchen to be a cosy hub of activity and thus fill it with warm reds and terra cottas, or you may wish to enhance a spacious kitchen by using pale greens and off-whites.

COMPLEMENTARY COLORS

The impact of any color can be increased dramatically by introducing the use of its complementary color, even if only in small quantities as an accent. For example, if orange is put next to blue, both colors will seem more pronounced: the orange will appear more orange and the blue will look bluer. Thus, in a kitchen which has been painted predominantly blue, orange or light wooden door knobs and moldings—and rows of cheery orange ceramic mugs and plates—would bring both colors alive.

An understanding of complementary colors can also be employed to bring out the latent undertones of a color. For example, brown has both latent green and red undertones (it is comprised of a mix of these two colors). Thus, the placement of green next to brown will bring out the red undertones; conversely, placing red next to brown will bring out the green undertones. In this way, complementary colors can be used to enhance one another.

THE LANGUAGE OF COLOR

Each color has its own levels of lightness, darkness, intensity, and opacity. A color can also be affected by the medium and method used to apply it. Here we demystify the language of color, to help you gain a better understanding of its elements.

TONE

Tone refers to the scale of light and dark in a color. Every color, or hue, has a range of tones. This is most easily seen on the scale of black to gray to white, yet all colors have this scale of relative lightness and darkness. If two colors have dissimilar tonal values, a sharp contrast can be seen between them; the tonal contrast between white and black shows this starkly. Tonal variations form the basis of monochromatic and contrasting color schemes.

INTENSITY

A color's intensity refers to its saturation. The idea of intensity is the basis for both broken color work and washes. Instead of lightening a color using white, it can be diluted to become a wash. If a wash of blue is added over white, for example, the blue will remain intense and vibrant, but the overall effect created will have a paler tone due to the white showing through. All colors can be lightened or darkened by altering the base color.

MEDIA

The type of medium used will affect the nature and character of a color, because it will alter the amount of light absorbed or given off by the finish. For example, a glossy, shiny painted surface will reflect light, allowing a solid black to be used without fear of creating too heavy or oppressive an effect. In contrast, a gloss varnish applied over a colorwash will result in the light bouncing off the effect, thereby obscuring its depth and luminosity. Flat, chalky colors—which are matte—will absorb light. Satin finishes or polishes give off a soft sheen that is perfect for bringing out the warm undertones in wood.

COLOR SCHEMES AND PALETTES

Students of interior design are often asked to create a "mood board," a collage of inspirational, interesting objects and colors gathered from anywhere and everywhere and then used to work toward a coherent color scheme. A collage based on this prototype will serve as an excellent tool to help you develop a color scheme for your kitchen. If you are unsure of which colors to use, give yourself a few days to collect color swatches, scraps of material, candy wrappers, wrapping paper, old photos, pages from magazines, and so on. Even a look at the clothing you buy, your linens, and other such personal purchases will reveal your preferences. Gather these items together to create your own "still life" to get a sense of how your preferred colors work together. Continue to discard from or add to your creation until you have decided on a color scheme. Generally speaking, kitchens call for simple color schemes—three "main" colors at the most is suggested. Feel free to use more than three colors, however, if they are tied together within a pattern.

▼ *Sleek, polished chrome and high-gloss granite are combined with flat gray walls and matte blue cupboards here for a clean, simple, modern look.*

Naturals & Off-whites

Naturals and off-whites increase the feeling of space, and introduce a light, airy feel. This palette ranges from the palest ivories and creams to deeper beiges, taupes and sandstones. It is important to use

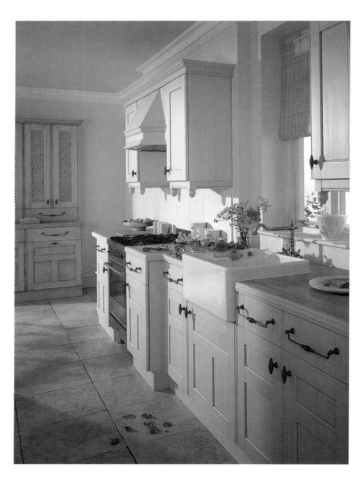

colors that are of a similar hue, but that have different tones, to avoid any possible color clashes. Cream and soft coffee shades are complementary, and create a peaceful mood and a contemporary style, while pale buff and sandstone shades lend a warm, country-style feel. When using naturals in larger spaces, add accents of contrasting or deeper colors, such as warm mochas, browns, or even black, to prevent the color scheme from appearing too bland. Natural fibers and textures are inherently suited to this palette—wood flooring or sisal and coir matting, bamboo and wooden blinds, and wicker baskets and drawers work especially well within this color scheme.

Relief impasto *stenciling*

A NEW TAKE on the well-known use of stencils, raised relief work is an impressively chic yet simple way to bring modern textured finishes into everyday surroundings. This effect can be used to imitate intricate carvings or moldings, adding style and elegance to flat or plain surfaces. It can also introduce a uniform theme into a kitchen with cupboard doors of different shapes and sizes.

Impasto, a thick, textured paint that produces a raised finish, and is relatively quick-drying, is used here. It can be painted, colorwashed, and sanded back to create a subtle, distressed look. Used in conjunction with metallic effects such as metal leaf or gilt creams, it can lend a lavish, sumptuous feel to a kitchen. Or, as shown here, it can be applied using a neutral color scheme for a simple, modern style.

MATERIALS AND TOOLS
ACRYLIC PRIMER
CREAM MATTE LATEX PAINT
IMPASTO PAINT, OR A THICK TEXTURED PAINT
PALE GRAY COLORWASH
2 HOUSEHOLD PAINTBRUSHES
VARNISH BRUSH
HOG-HAIR SOFTENER
DECORATORS' SPONGE
SHEET OF PAPER
BORDER OR LINEAR STENCIL
METAL RULER
PENCIL
LOW-TACK SPRAY ADHESIVE
OLD CREDIT CARD OR DECORATORS' STEEL FLOAT
FINE-GRADE SANDPAPER
MEDIUM-GRADE SANDPAPER
MATTE ACRYLIC VARNISH

1 • PREPARATION
This technique is only suitable for solid wooden and fiberboard doors—it will not work on melamine, vinyl, or laminate surfaces. Prepare the door following the instructions on pages 6-9, applying two coats of acrylic primer. Apply a coat of cream matte latex paint. When dry, sand using fine-grade sandpaper.

2 • MARKING UP
Choose a border or a linear stencil. On a paneled door, draw marks along the center of the outer panel with a pencil; on a plain door, the marks should be about $1\frac{1}{2}$–2 in (40–50mm) in from the edge. Make the same marks at intervals all around the door. Join the marks together to create a registration guide, to be lined up with the center of the stencil design.

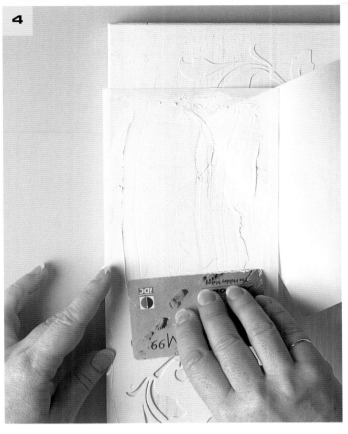

3 • STENCILING WITH IMPASTO

Decide how often you will need to repeat the stencil design, and at what intervals. Start stenciling in the middle of each length of the door. Spray the back of the stencil with low-tack spray adhesive, line it up with the registration guide, and affix it firmly to the door. Spoon 2 tsp (10ml) of impasto or a thick textured paint onto the edge of a credit card or a decorators' steel float. Pull the card lightly over the stencil at a 45-degree angle until the stencil is covered evenly. Gently peel away the stencil without disturbing the pattern created. Allow each stencil repeat to dry fully before stenciling the next.

4 • MITERING CORNERS

Miter each corner by positioning a sheet of paper at a 45-degree angle underneath the stencil—this will create a professional-looking, picture-frame corner. Allow each corner section to dry before stenciling the adjacent corner.

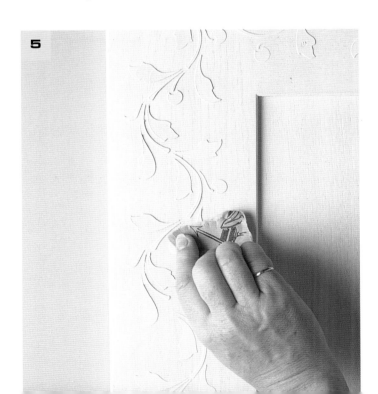

5 • SANDING ROUGH EDGES

When the stenciled sections are completely dry, lightly sand any rough sections of the raised stenciling using fine-grade sandpaper. Brush or vacuum away excess dust.

6 • OVERPAINTING

Apply a fine, even coat of cream matte latex paint over the entire door, taking care to brush out any excess paint that has gathered around the relief stencil design. Do not "overload" the paintbrush, or the fine detail of the relief motifs may be lost. Allow to dry thoroughly.

7 • COLORWASHING

Using a varnish brush, apply a coat of matte acrylic varnish over the door. This will create a non-absorbent base for the colorwash. Let the varnish dry thoroughly. Pour 1 tbsp (15ml) of pale gray colorwash onto a decorators' sponge, then spread over the door's surface using swirling movements. While the colorwash is still wet, lightly brush over it with a hog-hair softener in cross-hatching strokes to obtain a bloom of color.

8 • SANDING

When the colorwash is thoroughly dry, lightly sand the raised areas using medium-grade sandpaper. This will create a distressed effect, and will reveal the paler color of the impasto or thick textured paint underneath the colorwash. Do not over-sand, or the raised areas may be flattened.

TRADE SECRETS

- *If you make a mistake while the impasto or thick textured paint is still wet, simply wipe it away with a decorators' sponge. If you discover a mistake once the impasto has dried, just sand it down and try again.*

9 • FINISHING

Apply three coats of matte acrylic varnish, allowing each coat to dry thoroughly before applying the next. We use matte varnish here to enhance the natural chalkiness of this paint technique. The relief effect will be diminished if a gloss or eggshell (semi-gloss) varnish is used, as these add uniformity to or flatten raised objects.

HARDWARE

Plain white ceramic or painted and colorwashed knobs are a stylishly understated choice for this elegant finish.

Distressed paintwork
& hand-painted script

DECORATIVE LETTERING is an increasingly popular design element in modern and contemporary interiors. With a little time and patience, everyday items can be transformed into objects with real impact and lasting beauty using decorative scripts, which blend harmoniously with today's interiors, and have a timeless appeal. The ready availability of photocopiers, transfer paper, and sophisticated computer fonts means you don't need to be a budding calligrapher or an artist to achieve stunning effects. The subtle distressed paint finish shown here forms a stylish, simple base for a delicate calligraphic script—all in neutral, blending tones.

1 • PREPARATION AND BASE COAT

The distressing technique is only suitable for solid wood or fiberboard doors—it will not work on melamine, vinyl, or laminate surfaces. Prepare the surface following the instructions on pages 6-9. Load a household paintbrush liberally with smoky-brown wood paint, and spread it over the surface in crisscross strokes. Wipe excess paint from the brush, then work back over the surface again, using upward and downward strokes to ensure a smooth, even coverage.

2 • APPLYING THE WAX RESIST

Distressing creates the natural look of a surface gently worn by the passing of time. For maximum effect, concentrate on those areas where wear-and-tear is most likely to have occurred. Rub a household candle along the door's moldings, corners, and edges, and also onto some of its flat areas, ensuring a good build-up of wax. Once applied, the wax acts as a "resist," allowing the top layer of paint to be rubbed back to reveal the original color underneath.

MATERIALS AND TOOLS

SMOKY-BROWN HIGHLY PIGMENTED WOOD PAINT
IVORY HIGHLY PIGMENTED WOOD PAINT
GOLD STENCIL PAINT OR ARTISTS' ACRYLIC PAINT
2 HOUSEHOLD PAINTBRUSHES
VARNISH BRUSH
FINE AND MEDIUM ARTISTS' SABLE BRUSHES
PAINT MIXING PALETTE
PAPER TOWEL
HOUSEHOLD CANDLE
PHOTOCOPIED SCRIPTS
LOW-TACK SPRAY ADHESIVE
PAPER SHEETS CUT TO SIZE OF DOOR
TRANSFER PAPER CUT TO SIZE OF DOOR
SHARP, HARD PENCIL
PLASTIC OR GUM ERASER
MEDIUM-GRADE SANDPAPER
FINE-GRADE SANDPAPER
MATTE OR SEMI-GLOSS ACRYLIC VARNISH

4 • DISTRESSING THE FINISH

Use medium-grade sandpaper to rub back the areas where the candle wax was applied—the paint will appear sticky, lumpy, or darker in these areas—to reveal the base coat beneath. Once all the wax has been removed and the desired effect has been achieved, rub the entire door down with fine-grade sandpaper. This will eliminate any bumps and will leave a smooth working surface for the next stage, the hand-painting.

3 • APPLYING THE TOP COAT

Using smooth, even strokes, apply two or three coats of ivory wood paint to the door, allowing it to dry between coats. Several coats will be needed because the top coat color is lighter than the base coat. The paint may become a little bumpy over the waxed areas; this will be sanded back when the distressing is done.

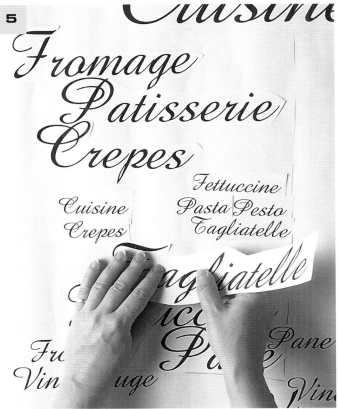

5 • DESIGNING AND LAYING OUT THE DECORATIVE SCRIPT

Choose text and a decorative script that suits the style of your kitchen. In this example, a calligraphy script from a computer font has been used to style some familiar Italian and French words on a food theme. The text has then been printed out at three different sizes; or you can print out at one size and enlarge or reduce on a photocopier. Cut out your selection of words and, using a low-tack spray adhesive, stick them in the desired order onto a sheet of paper the same size as the door, to create a paper template.

6 • TRANSFERRING THE DESIGN TO THE DOOR

Lay a sheet of transfer paper on the door. Remove one word at a time from your paper template, and lay it on top of the transfer paper, in the same position on the door as it occupies on your template. Using a sharp, hard pencil, carefully draw around the outline of each letter. The paper will transfer the design to the door, creating an outline ready for painting. Repeat with each word.

7 • PAINTING THE SCRIPT

The best effect is achieved by using colors that are similar in tone: strongly contrasting colors will make the script appear to leap off the door. Mix the two wood paint colors to create a pale beige-brown and a cream. Using artists' sable brushes, paint the largest words in beige-brown, the medium-sized words in cream, and the smallest words in gold artists' acrylic or stencil paint. Let dry.

8 • FINISHING

Use a plastic or gum eraser to remove any lines or marks left by the transfer paper or pencil. Brush away the dust. Use a varnish brush to apply a coat of matte acrylic varnish over the entire door. Take care not to overwork the varnish in case it lifts the decorative script. When completely dry, apply two more coats, for extra protection. A semi-gloss acrylic varnish can be used if a semi-sheen finish is preferred.

TRADE SECRETS

- *When transferring the design to the door, work from the top left to bottom right if you are right-handed, or from the top right to bottom left if you are left-handed. This reduces the chance of smudging the transferred design.*

- *Mix the paint for the lettering to the consistency of light cream. This will make application easier, and ensure good coverage.*

HARDWARE

The design is complemented perfectly by simple wooden knobs that have been given a distressed finish, as described above.

Victorian cookbook-style *decoupage*

DECOUPAGE—THE ART of decorating surfaces with paper cutouts—has long been used to embellish screens and small pieces of furniture, and was a particular favorite among Victorian ladies who spent many a happy afternoon decoupaging objects as keepsakes. Here we adapt the craft, aptly using Victorian cookbook-style motifs applied in a modern collage to create a design suitable for the kitchen. An easy and inexpensive technique, decoupage is an effective way to add interest and charm to any kitchen.

MATERIALS AND TOOLS
IVORY MATTE LATEX PAINT
WHITE WATER-BASED UNIVERSAL TINTER
HOUSEHOLD PAINTBRUSH
3 VARNISH BRUSHES
2 FITCH BRUSHES
PHOTOCOPIED MOTIFS
IVORY TISSUE PAPER
NEWSPAPER
SCISSORS
WATER-BASED WHITE GLUE
FINE-GRADE SANDPAPER (FOR A WOODEN DOOR)
WHITE SHELLAC
BUTTON POLISH SHELLAC, OR WHITE SHELLAC TINTED
WITH BURNT SIENNA, YELLOW OCHER, AND RAW
UMBER TO PRODUCE A GOLDEN BROWN
MATTE ACRYLIC VARNISH

1 • PREPARATION
Prepare a solid wood, fiberboard, vinyl, melamine or laminate surface following the instructions on pages 6-9. Apply two coats of ivory matte latex paint, letting the first coat dry before applying the second. Sand between coats using fine-grade sandpaper on a wooden door only. Choose a selection of motifs from a decoupage source book or a favorite recipe book; wrapping paper decorated with a food theme will work equally well. Make color photocopies of the motifs you wish to use.

2 • APPLYING SHELLAC TO THE MOTIFS
Lay the photocopied motifs on newspaper. Use a varnish brush to paint a coat of white shellac over them, brushing it on in even strokes. The shellac seals the images, making them easy to cut and tear. Prepare plenty of motifs in this way, so you will have a good selection to choose from for your design. Allow to dry fully.

4 • STICKING DOWN THE TISSUE PAPER

Add a little water to some water-based white glue until it is the consistency of light cream—if the glue is too runny, the paper will wrinkle as it dries. Paint the diluted glue onto the door with a fitch brush, then smooth the tissue paper into place with your fingertips. The tissue paper will naturally wrinkle in places; press the wrinkles down to add texture.

3 • LAYING OUT THE COLLAGE

Tear some strips of ivory tissue paper—these will act as an underlayer to the collage—and put aside. Cut out those sections or details of the motifs that you wish to use; tear others, for a different effect. Lay the motifs on the door, moving them around until you find an arrangement you like. Lay the pieces of the final design aside in the desired order, so they will be easily transferable, in this order, for gluing.

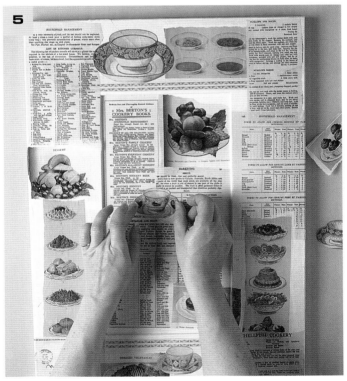

5 • STICKING DOWN THE COLLAGE

Working on one section of the door at a time, apply white glue to the back of each motif with the fitch brush, and press them firmly onto the door with your fingertips. Smooth over each motif to avoid wrinkling. Continue gluing and smoothing out wrinkles until the decoupage is complete. Allow the glue to dry completely.

6

TRADE SECRETS

- *Keep the images and colors linked, either by theme or color, to keep the design from looking too busy.*

- *When sticking down the photocopied motifs, work on one section at a time. This will ensure that the collage remains accurate to the layout previously prepared.*

- *As the glue dries, it may wrinkle the paper motifs. Try to smooth out any air bubbles as they appear.*

6 • APPLYING BUTTON POLISH SHELLAC

Use a varnish brush to apply a coat of button polish shellac, or white shellac tinted to a golden brown, to seal the decoupage and add a honey-colored antiqued look to the door. Allow to dry thoroughly.

7

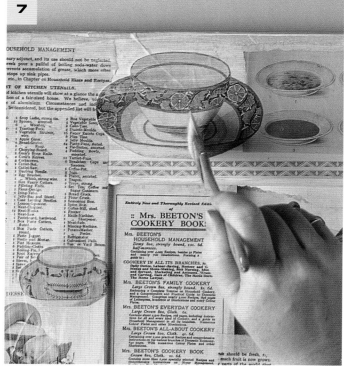

HARDWARE

A plain wooden knob, either new or antique, would be a suitably simple addition to this fun, ecclectic design.

7 • FINISHING

Add two drops of white water-based universal tinter to some matte acrylic varnish, and apply three coats with a varnish brush, allowing each coat to dry fully before applying the next.

Neutral territory

The soft, delicate shades and subtle color combinations of the natural and off-white palette are shown here in a range of different techniques and color pairings. Cool coffee-and-cream crackle glaze, colorwash in warm, sandstone hues, and rag-rolling in gentle creams are just a few of the designs that suit this color palette particularly well.

▲ **COFFEE-AND-CREAM CRACKLE GLAZE**
The subtle use of crackle glaze paired with soft coffee and cream colors creates a cool, contemporary style. After priming (see pages 6–9), paint the inner panel with two coats of mocha coffee matte latex or wood paint, and the outer panel with two coats of creamy coffee matte latex or wood paint. When dry, mask off the outer panel, then vertically brush crackle glaze onto the inner panel. Mix the two paints together to create a third, mid-tone color, and paint horizontally over the dry crackle glaze, taking care not to brush over the same area twice. Once dry, seal with two coats of matte polyurethane varnish (see Polyurethane varnish, page 23).
Suitable for all surfaces.

◀ **WILLOW-LEAF DECOUPAGE**
This delicate design creates a restful, natural feel. After priming (see pages 6–9), apply two coats of ivory matte latex or wood paint. Use diluted water-based white glue to stick the leaf skeletons firmly onto the door (see Step 5, page 39). Seal with white shellac, then apply three coats of matte acrylic varnish.
Suitable for wooden and fiberboard surfaces.

▼ **CHECKED COLORWASH**

A sandstone colorwash applied in large checks creates this warm look. After priming (see pages 6–9), apply two coats of non-absorbent off-white matte latex paint or matte latex paint sealed with matte acrylic varnish. When dry, stick down horizontal rows of low-tack painters' tape at 4 in (100mm) and 1 in (25mm) intervals. Mix a sandstone colorwash, then wash over the door (see Colorwashing, page 18). After 10 minutes, apply a stony-gray colorwash and drag through it following the thin tape lines (see Liquid glaze effects, page 19). When dry, stick down vertical rows of low-tack painters' tape at the same intervals and repeat the colorwashing process. Remove the tape. After 24 hours, apply three coats of matte acrylic varnish.

Suitable for all surfaces.

▲ **FROSTED-GLASS STENCIL**

Glass doors get a new look with this simple faux etched and stenciled technique. Mask off the glass panel, prime the door frame (see pages 6–9), and apply two coats of milky chocolate matte latex paint. Remove the tape. Draw a selection of leaf motifs on a stencil card, cut them out, then stick them onto the glass using low-tack adhesive spray, leaving spaces in between them. Mix a bit of white matte latex paint into some frosting medium and stipple around the leaves (see Step 6, page 49). When dry, carefully peel off the leaf motifs.

Suitable for clear glass-paneled doors with any type of frame.

▼ **SANDSTONE SPECKLE**
This technique recreates the grainy texture of stone. After priming (see pages 6–9), apply two coats of cream matte latex or wood paint. Mix four slightly different stone-colored glazes to the consistency of milk, tinting them with varying amounts of raw umber, burnt sienna, and yellow ocher (see Liquid glaze effects, page 19). Mask off the outer panel and loosely paint the lightest glaze onto the inner panel. Stipple (see page 19), then spatter the remaining glazes (see Step 6, page 95). After 24 hours, apply three coats of matte acrylic varnish.
Suitable for all surfaces.

▲ **FILIGREE LEAF DESIGN**
A delicate filigree and distressed design. The door does not need priming. Rub candle wax onto parts of the door, then apply two coats of cream matte latex or wood paint. When dry, distress the moldings and edges using coarse-grade sandpaper (see Distressing, page 18), then smooth with fine-grade sandpaper. Cut a piece of white card to fit the inner panel and coat the card with button polish shellac (or raw umber-tinted white shellac). Transfer a leaf design to the back of the card (see Step 6, page 36) and cut out using a craft knife. Discard the leaf shape and leave the negative image. Apply a second coat of button polish shellac to the cutout. When dry, brush diluted water-based white glue onto the inner panel. When tacky, smooth the cutout onto the panel, pressing firmly to avoid wrinkles. After one hour, seal with white shellac; apply a second coat after two hours. Leave overnight. Apply three coats of semi-gloss acrylic varnish.
Suitable for wooden surfaces.

▼ CREAM RAG-ROLL

A contemporary use of the rag-rolling technique. After priming (see pages 6–9), apply two coats of magnolia-white matte latex paint. Mask off the dry outer panel. Paint the inner panel with pale yellow satin latex paint. Mix up a coffee cream glaze using ⅓ glazing liquid, ⅓ magnolia-white latex paint and ⅓ acrylic semi-gloss varnish to the consistency of light cream, and tint with raw umber, yellow ocher, and burnt sienna. Dip a rag into the glaze and roll over the panel (see Liquid glaze effects, page 19). When dry, remove the tape and apply three coats of matte acrylic varnish.
Suitable for all surfaces.

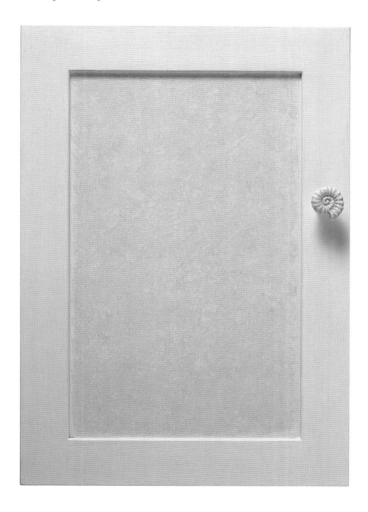

▲ PEN AND INK BARLEY STIPPLE

This barley motif brings a country feel to the kitchen. After priming (see pages 6–9), apply two coats of cream matte latex or wood paint. Mix equal proportions of colorwash and matte acrylic varnish (see Colorwashing, page 18) and tint to a warm sandstone using raw umber, burnt sienna, and yellow ocher. Brush onto the door and stipple (see Liquid glaze effects, page 19); seal with matte acrylic varnish. Draw a barley design on transfer paper and transfer the design to the door (see Step 6, page 36). Go over the design with a black, fine, permanent, waterproof fibertip pen. Dilute black wood paint with water and apply as a wash over parts of the motif to soften the design. Also add some sandstone as a thin wash. Create a border with two rows of low-tack painters' tape and fill in with black paint. When dry, remove the tape and glide white shellac over the design. Apply three coats of semi-gloss acrylic varnish to the entire door.
Suitable for all surfaces.

YELLOWS & BROWNS

ONE OF THE MOST DIVERSE COLORS IN THE DECORATOR'S PALETTE, YELLOW LENDS ITSELF TO A HOST OF TREATMENTS AND STYLES. ORANGEY-YELLOW SHADES BRING A SENSE OF LIVELINESS AND WARMTH TO A ROOM, ILLUMINATING SMALL OR DREARY SPACES AND ENLIVENING BRIGHT, AIRY ONES. DUE TO THEIR HIGHER REFLECTIVE VALUE, PALER SHADES OF YELLOW OPEN UP SMALLER AREAS AND GIVE THEM A CHEERFUL LIFT. VIRTUALLY ALL SHADES WITHIN THE YELLOW PALETTE CAN BE MATCHED WITH A WIDE VARIETY OF OTHER COLORS— WHITE, RED, BLUE, GREEN, AND BLACK ARE SOME OF THE MOST POPULAR COMBINATIONS FOR THE KITCHEN. GOLD DETAILS OR ACCESSORIES AGAINST A YELLOW BACKGROUND ADD A HINT OF OPULENCE. TOWARD THE DARKER END OF THE SPECTRUM, THE USE OF NATURAL EARTH COLORS, WOODSY TONES AND HONEY BROWNS IN A KITCHEN WILL IMBUE A SENSE OF WARMTH, COZINESS, AND COMFORT.

Vine-leaf *stipple*

3

THIS EFFECT IS BASED ON the Victorian technique of "fernwork," the fashion of stippling onto bare wood using an arrangement of leaves as natural stencils. When the leaf shapes are removed, their silhouettes reveal the wood beneath.

We recreate this look here in a style that is both delicate and striking, using colors that result in an ambience ideal for kitchens lacking in warmth or character. Our design is based on the attractive vine-shaped leaves of *Parthenocissus*, or Virginia creeper, which lend themselves perfectly to this treatment. We have used a bare, sanded oak door, warmed up first with a honey-colored polish, and finished with tawny and chestnut glazes. Different leaf shapes can be used; delicate and frond-like leaves tend to give the most pleasing effect.

MATERIALS AND TOOLS

WATER-BASED UNIVERSAL TINTERS: BURNT SIENNA, RAW UMBER, YELLOW OCHER

RED ARTISTS' ACRYLIC PAINT

2 VARNISH BRUSHES

2 STENCIL BRUSHES

3 FINE ARTISTS' SABLE BRUSHES

SELECTION OF LEAVES

MAGAZINE OR NEWSPAPER

SEVERAL BOOKS OR OTHER HEAVY, FLAT OBJECTS

2 PAINT PAILS

LOW-TACK SPRAY ADHESIVE

PAPER TOWEL

2 ELASTIC BANDS

CRAFT KNIFE

FINE-GRADE SANDPAPER

ACRYLIC GLAZING LIQUID

BUTTON POLISH SHELLAC, OR WHITE SHELLAC TINTED WITH BURNT SIENNA, YELLOW OCHER, AND RAW UMBER TO PRODUCE A GOLDEN BROWN

SEMI-GLOSS ACRYLIC OR OIL-BASED VARNISH

1 • PREPARATION

This technique works best on bare, sanded, solid woods, such as oak or pine, but it can also be applied on painted wood, fiberboard, melamine, vinyl, or laminate surfaces, although these will have less of a natural "woodsy" appearance when finished. Prepare the surface following the instructions on pages 6-9. A few days prior to beginning, collect the leaves you intend to use and press them between the pages of a magazine or newspaper, weighted down under several books or other heavy, flat objects. Sand the door well, using fine-grade sandpaper.

2 • MIXING THE GLAZES

Just before you start, mix up a warm chestnut glaze and a lighter, tawny glaze as follows. Pour 4 tsp (20ml) of acrylic glazing liquid and 2 tsp (10ml) of water into each of two separate paint pails. To make the chestnut glaze, add several drops of burnt sienna and raw umber; for the tawny glaze, add a few drops of yellow ocher, and some burnt sienna and raw umber. Stir the glazes well, ensuring that the colorant is fully dispersed.

3 • SEALING THE WOOD

Using a varnish brush, carefully apply a coat of button polish shellac, or white shellac tinted golden brown, over the door's entire surface. Use long, even brushstrokes, letting the polish "glide" over the surface. Take care not to overwork any one area—shellac is fast-drying, and quickly becomes tacky, so overbrushing will result in a rough, sticky surface. The polish seals the wood and adds a warm tone that suits this design. When fully dry, use fine-grade sandpaper to rub down any grain raised by the shellac. Brush or wipe away the sanding dust.

4 • CREATING THE DESIGN

Carefully remove the leaves, which should now be completely flat, from their makeshift press. Lay them out on the door in an arrangement you like. We used whole leaves of varying sizes for the central panel, and broke off single leaflets for the outer panel.

6 • STIPPLING ON THE GLAZES

Pour some of each glaze into separate saucers. Dip a dry stencil brush into the chestnut glaze, wiping off any excess on a paper towel. Wrap an elastic band around the base of the bristles for more control. Stipple—dabbing the brush onto the surface—the chestnut glaze around the leaves in the central panel, until the wood is covered. Do the same using the tawny glaze around the leaves on the outer panel.

5 • FIXING THE LEAVES

Remove a few leaves from a small section of the door. Spray them lightly with low-tack spray adhesive, and smooth each leaf back into position on the door. Move on to the next section, and continue carefully like this until all the leaves have been stuck down in position on the door.

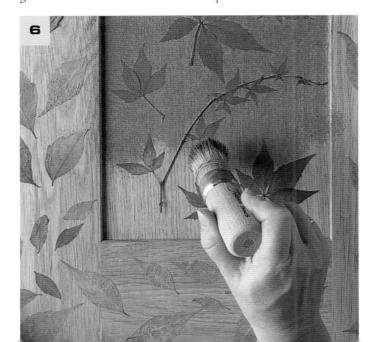

7 • REMOVING THE LEAVES

As soon as all areas of the wood have been stippled, you can begin removing the leaves. Using a fingernail, or the pointed end of a craft knife, carefully pull up the tip of each leaf, then peel it back. If any leaves appear to be stuck, do not spend too long trying to remove them—peel off the remaining ones, then go back to the difficult ones and use a craft knife to lift or scrape them away.

8 • HAND-PAINTING

Any leaf shapes that appear blurred can now be touched up; use a fine artists' sable brush to paint in the missing detail with the appropriate glaze. Next, mix red artists' acrylic paint with some chestnut glaze, and paint in the rim between the central panel and the outer panel. Allow to dry fully.

9 • FINISHING

Apply another coat of button polish shellac, or white shellac tinted golden brown, gliding it onto the door surface without overworking it. Once this has dried, you may need to sand the door lightly with fine-grade sandpaper for a completely smooth surface. Brush or vacuum away excess dust. Finish by varnishing with three coats of semi-gloss acrylic or oil-based varnish, allowing each coat to dry thoroughly before applying the next. If using oil-based varnish, sand lightly between coats.

TRADE SECRETS

- *Leaves that cannot be removed with a craft knife will loosen when dabbed with a cotton swab soaked in whatever solvent is recommended on the spray adhesive's label. Take care not to disturb the surrounding glaze.*

- *You may decide to hand-paint some detail, but resist the temptation to paint in the leaf veins. Doing so will make the design look fussy, and detract from the simplicity of the image.*

HARDWARE

A shellacked wooden knob, perhaps decorated with a leaf motif, or a simple wrought-iron handle would work well with this design.

Textured *combing*

A MODERN INTERPRETATION of combing glazes, this effect will add a wonderfully rich texture to the surfaces of your cupboard doors, creating an overall look of contemporary chic. Simple to achieve, this technique involves applying a thick, paste-like paint onto a previously painted surface, and combing through it to reveal the color beneath. This effect works especially well on doors that have an inner panel.

The use of different color combinations will produce radically different effects; loud, bright colors will naturally create a very different look than softer, more muted tones. Here we use a combination of mochas, creams, and browns, which blend together harmoniously to produce a soft corduroy look.

MATERIALS AND TOOLS

MOCHA BROWN LATEX PAINT
CREAM MATTE LATEX PAINT
COMBING PASTE OR CREAM LATEX PAINT MIXED WITH
IMPASTO (OR SIMILARLY THICK TEXTURED PAINT),
AND ACRYLIC GLAZING LIQUID
WATER-BASED UNIVERSAL TINTERS OR ARTISTS'
ACRYLIC PAINTS: BURNT UMBER, YELLOW OCHER,
WHITE
2 HOUSEHOLD PAINTBRUSHES
ARTISTS' SABLE BRUSH
VARNISH BRUSH
LOW-TACK PAINTERS' TAPE
⅜ IN (10MM) LOW-TACK LINING TAPE
PAINT PAIL
RUBBER DECORATING COMB
FINE-GRADE SANDPAPER
MATTE ACRYLIC VARNISH
SEMI-GLOSS ACRYLIC VARNISH (OPTIONAL)

1 • PREPARATION

This technique is only suitable for solid wood and fiberboard doors—it is not appropriate for melamine, vinyl, or laminate doors. Prepare the surface following the instructions on page 6-9. Apply two coats of mocha brown latex paint, allowing plenty of time for drying in between, and sanding between coats using fine-grade sandpaper. When dry, use a varnish brush to apply a coat of matte acrylic varnish. Allow to dry, then mask off the molding and outer panel with low-tack painters' tape.

2 • MIXING THE PASTE

If you are using a ready-made combing paste, tint it with white, burnt umber and yellow ocher water-based universal tinters or artists' acrylic paints to produce a soft cream color. If a ready-made paste is unavailable, you can create a similar mixture using one part cream matte latex paint, one part impasto (or similarly thick textured paint), and one part acrylic glazing liquid. Tint this mixture as described above. Make sure that either mixture is adequately stirred.

3 • APPLYING THE PASTE

Using a household paintbrush, apply a thick, even layer of combing paste to the door's inner panel using smooth vertical brushstrokes. Make sure that the paste is distributed evenly over the panel.

4 • COMBING

Working on one door at a time, begin combing immediately after the paste has been applied. Starting at the left side of the panel, grip the comb with both hands and drag it down through the paste. Exert a firm, even pressure, keeping the movement as straight as possible. As you comb down through each section, overlap the comb's teeth by one notch, and repeat the same dragging action, until the entire inner panel has been combed. Leave to dry for at least 24 hours at room temperature, then carefully peel back the painters' tape.

TRADE SECRETS

- *When pulling the comb downward, try to do so in a straight line. Do not worry if the lines are slightly imperfect, however; lines that are gently wavy can enhance the overall effect.*

- *Make sure to tint the combing paste with a substantial amount of color, especially white, to ensure opacity.*

5 • FRAMING THE INNER PANEL

Frame the textured inner panel by hand-painting a cream line at the edge of the door's molding. Affix two lines of $\frac{3}{8}$ in (10mm) low-tack lining tape to the edge of the molding, about $\frac{1}{4}$ in (6mm) apart. Using an artists' sable brush, apply two coats of cream matte latex paint between the tape lines, allowing the first coat to dry before painting the second. When the paint has dried, carefully remove the tape.

6 • FINISHING

Using a varnish brush, apply three coats of matte acrylic varnish, allowing each coat to dry thoroughly before applying the next. Or, if you wish to soften the textured look further, use a semi-gloss acrylic varnish to achieve a flatter, more unified effect.

HARDWARE

Complement this finish with a simple bronze or brass handle or knob—the contrasting smoothness will highlight the rich texture.

Birch wood graining
with *faux ebony & ivory inlay*

AUX WOOD GRAINING is an established way of transforming inexpensive and unexciting pieces of furniture and plywood panels into stylish, expensive-looking items. Imitations of pale wood grains such as maple and birch are particularly fashionable for contemporary kitchen spaces, creating an ambience that is crisp and bright, as well as elegant and stylish.

Inexpensive and simple to achieve, this technique offers a fabulous solution to converting dull and lifeless kitchen cabinets into modern, exciting ones. To complete this look, embellish the grained surface with a thin black and white line painted to look like ebony and ivory inlay.

MATERIALS AND TOOLS
IVORY MATTE LATEX PAINT OR HIGHLY PIGMENTED WOOD PAINT

WATER-BASED UNIVERSAL TINTERS: YELLOW OCHER, RAW UMBER, BURNT SIENNA, WHITE

ARTISTS' ACRYLIC PAINTS: WHITE, BLACK

2 HOUSEHOLD PAINTBRUSHES

VARNISH BRUSH

FLOGGING BRUSH

PENCIL OVERGRAINER

BADGER-HAIR SOFTENER

3 FINE ARTISTS' SABLE BRUSHES

½ IN (13MM) ONE-STROKE BRUSH, SABLE OR NYLON

METAL RULER

PENCIL

½ IN (13MM) LOW-TACK LINING OR PAINTERS' TAPE

PAINT PAIL

FINE-GRADE SANDPAPER

ACRYLIC GLAZING LIQUID

SEMI-GLOSS ACRYLIC VARNISH

MATTE ACRYLIC VARNISH

1 • PREPARATION
This treatment can be used on fiberboard, melamine, vinyl, laminate, and closed-grained wooden doors (an open grain should be filled and sanded—see page 9).

Prepare the surface following the instructions on pages 6-9. Apply two coats of ivory matte latex paint or wood paint, leaving the first coat to dry completely before applying the second. Sand lightly between coats using fine-grade sandpaper on a wooden door only. Paint as evenly as possible—it is important to obtain a flat, smooth surface. When completely dry, use a varnish brush to apply a coat of semi-gloss acrylic varnish. Allow to dry thoroughly.

2 • APPLYING THE FIRST GLAZE
Mix up a pale creamy glaze as follows: spoon two parts acrylic glazing liquid into a paint pail, and make up the final third with equal parts of water and matte acrylic varnish. Tint with two to three drops of yellow ocher, one drop of raw umber, one drop of burnt sienna, and two drops of white water-based universal tinter. Paint on the glaze using loose brushstrokes.

3 • FLOGGING AND OVERGRAINING

Take the flogging brush and, working from the bottom of the door upward, flog over the still-wet glaze—hitting the brush flatly onto the surface—until a consistent, flecked effect has been achieved. Pull the pencil overgrainer down through the damp glaze in wavy lines, repeatedly wiping the excess glaze from the brush. Soften with the badger-hair softener, brushing lightly in all directions. Allow to dry thoroughly.

TRADE SECRETS

- *When painting wood-grain finishes, obtain a sample or photograph of the wood you are recreating to use as a reference, and practice the technique on cardboard before working directly on the actual surface.*

- *Keep all grain lines and mottling patterns as simple and subtle as possible: remember that "less is more."*

4 • PAINTING IN THE GRAIN

Mix up a mid-tone brown glaze using the same proportions of glazing liquid, water and matte acrylic varnish as in the first glaze, and, using universal tinters, tint with one drop of burnt sienna, one drop of yellow ocher, and half a drop of raw umber. Using a fine artists' sable brush, paint in the lighter lines of the grain with this glaze. Loosely follow the lines created by the pencil overgrainer, softening frequently with the badger-hair softener. The lines should be long and tapering, traveling the width or length of each panel, with occasional "heart grain" shapes. Refer to real birch for inspiration.

HARDWARE

A slender brass handle or a plain black knob would best suit this effect.

5 • MOTTLING

Dilute the mid-tone brown glaze used for the grain lines with water to make a transparent wash. Use a ½ in (13mm) one-stroke brush to apply a small amount of this wash in short, soft marks, at a horizontal angle to a few of the grain lines—like a subtle zebra print. Soften these marks with the softener as you work. Add a tapering shadow to the "heart grain" shapes; this will make the grain lines appear less distinct, lending extra depth. Allow to dry for at least 24 hours. Apply a coat of semi-gloss acrylic varnish to seal and protect, and allow to dry for another 24 hours.

6 • CREATING THE FAUX INLAY

Draw a fine pencil guideline through the middle of the outer panel of the door, all the way around the door. Use a ruler to ensure straight lines. Stick a strip of ½ in (13mm) low-tack lining or painters' tape on both sides of the guideline, leaving a ¼ in (6mm) gap. Using an artists' sable brush, paint in the line with white artists' acrylic paint. Allow to dry thoroughly.

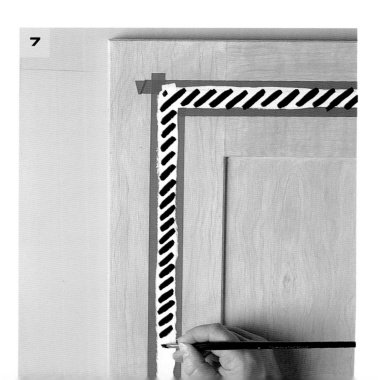

7 • COMPLETING THE FAUX INLAY

Add small black diagonal flecks to the white line using black artists' acrylic paint, creating equal diagonal lines of black and white. Carefully peel off the tapes, and leave until completely dry.

8 • FINISHING

Apply three coats of semi-gloss acrylic varnish to seal and protect, allowing each coat to dry thoroughly before applying the next.

Gold *craquelure*

GOLD ALWAYS EXUDES WARMTH when used in interiors, but it can sometimes be a little overbearing and grand for its surroundings. To lighten the look, gold can be used as an embellishment to a lighter color scheme, combining modern materials and traditional styles, as we have done here. The result is a charming kitchen design possessing both the richness of gold and a subtlety of color. When applied to an entire kitchen, this color scheme creates a warm, elegant ambience while still retaining a sense of comfort and spaciousness.

MATERIALS AND TOOLS

IVORY MATTE LATEX PAINT OR HIGHLY PIGMENTED WOOD PAINT

SAND SUEDE-EFFECT PAINT OR MATTE HIGHLY PIGMENTED WOOD PAINT

GOLD ARTISTS' OIL PAINT

YELLOW OCHER WATER-BASED UNIVERSAL TINTER

2 HOUSEHOLD PAINTBRUSHES

5 VARNISH BRUSHES

LOW-TACK PAINTERS' TAPE

LINT-FREE CLOTH

WHITE SPIRIT (OPTIONAL)

PAINT PAIL

FINE-GRADE SANDPAPER

WHITE SHELLAC

TWO-PART CRAQUELURE VARNISH

SEMI-GLOSS ACRYLIC VARNISH

METALLIC ACRYLIC VARNISH

1 • PREPARATION

This technique is only suitable for solid wood and fiberboard doors—it will not work on melamine, vinyl, or laminate surfaces. Prepare the surface following the instructions on pages 6-9. Apply two coats of ivory matte latex paint or wood paint to the inner panel, letting the first coat dry before applying the second, and sanding between coats using fine-grade sandpaper. Allow to dry thoroughly.

2 • PAINTING THE BORDER

Use low-tack painters' tape to mask off the inner panel. Paint the outer panel with sand suede-effect paint; if this type of paint is not available, use a very matte wood paint. Leave until completely dry.

3 • APPLYING THE VARNISH

Remove the painters' tape from the inner panel and mask off the outer panel. Using a varnish brush, apply the first step of the craquelure varnish. Brush it on evenly, making sure no corners or edges have been missed. Allow to dry completely.

Paint on the second step of the varnish with a new varnish brush, brushing on a medium-thick, even coat. Leave overnight to dry completely.

4 • HIGHLIGHTING THE CRACKS

Squeeze some gold artists' oil paint onto a lint-free cloth and rub it over the dry craquelure, making sure it gets into all the cracks. Rub back the oil paint with a clean cloth so that the color remains in the cracks only. You will need to switch to a new clean cloth several times. If the oil paint remains steadfast, pour a small amount of white spirit onto a clean cloth and rub it lightly over the surface, leaving the gold in the cracks intact. Rub down again with a clean cloth. Allow to dry for 24 hours.

5 • SEALING AND VARNISHING

Using a new varnish brush, seal the craquelure panel with a coat of white shellac. Once this has dried, apply three coats of semi-gloss acrylic varnish, allowing each coat to dry thoroughly before applying the next.

TRADE SECRETS

- *Do not confuse crackle glaze and craquelure varnishes. Craquelure is a two-step varnish that produces hairline cracks in the varnish coat, while crackle glaze is sandwiched between two layers of paint, and causes the top coat of paint to crack.*

- *The size of the cracks made by craquelure varnish will be determined by the thickness of the second coat. Brush the varnish on thickly to achieve larger cracks, or apply a thinner coat for smaller cracks.*

6 • APPLYING TINTED METALLIC VARNISH

Pour some metallic acrylic varnish into a paint pail, and tint with two drops of yellow ocher water-based universal tinter. Stir thoroughly. Mask off the inner panel, and, using a new varnish brush, paint the tinted metallic varnish onto the outer panel using smooth, even strokes. This final touch will give the door frame a beautiful gold, pearlescent luster.

HARDWARE
Antiqued brass or gold knobs and fittings mirror the richness, opulence, and warmth of the gold hue.

Sunny side up

Here we see the remarkable versatility of the yellow and brown palette. Some of the most beautiful techniques in this color range are shown here, including a sunny yellow plaster finish, decoupage and craquelure in warm orange tones, and luxurious gold effects.

▲ LINEN STENCIL AND EMBROIDERY SAMPLER

The golden amber tones of this effect create a warming ambience. After priming (see pages 6–9), apply two coats of pale yellow matte latex or wood paint to the outer panel and warm orange to the inner panel. When dry, stencil warm orange through a fine mesh linen stencil on the outer panel, working in circular strokes. Seal a color photocopy of a yellow or an orange embroidery sampler with white shellac; when dry, cut to fit the door panel. Stick the photocopy smoothly onto the panel with diluted water-based white glue (see Step 5, page 39). When dry, apply button polish shellac (or raw umber-tinted white shellac) to the whole door. After 24 hours, apply semi-gloss polyurethane varnish (see Polyurethane varnish, page 23).

Suitable for all surfaces.

◀ POLISHED PLASTER AND STENCIL

The luster of polished plaster tinted warm yellow is highlighted with a sophisticated black border stencil. After priming (see pages 6–9), apply two coats of yellow matte latex paint. Tint some polished plaster with yellow (see Step 2, page 76) and apply a fine layer to the surface; remove the excess, then smooth out (see Step 3, page 77). Apply a second coat. When nearly dry, polish to a sheen (see Step 4, page 77). Stencil translucent (diluted) black paint through a border stencil, mitering the corners (see Step 4, page 31). When dry, apply liquid wax and buff (see Liquid waxes, page 23), or semi-gloss acrylic varnish if the door is near a sink area.

Suitable for wooden and fiberboard surfaces.

▼ **DECOUPAGE AND CRAQUELURE**

A warm, rustic, country-style design. After priming (see pages 6–9), apply two coats of matte cream-colored non-absorbent latex paint or latex paint sealed with matte acrylic varnish, then wash over with a terra cotta colorwash (see Colorwashing, page 18). After 24 hours, seal with matte acrylic varnish. Seal fruit decoupage motifs with white shellac and cut out (see Step 5, page 39). Stick the motifs onto the inner panel with diluted water-based white glue (see Step 2, page 38). Seal with button polish shellac (or raw umber-tinted white shellac). When dry, mask off the outer panel and apply both steps of the craquelure varnish to the inner panel. When dry, rub raw umber artists' oil paint into the cracks (see Steps 3 and 4, page 61). After 24 hours, seal with white shellac. Remove the tape. Apply three coats of matte acrylic varnish.
Suitable for all surfaces.

▲ **YELLOW COLORWASH AND SUNFLOWER STAMP**

Cheery sunflowers on a yellow colorwashed background create a lively, radiant look. After priming (see pages 6–9), apply two coats of non-absorbent warm yellow matte latex paint or matte latex paint sealed with matte acrylic varnish, then wash with a bright yellow ocher-colored colorwash (see Color-washing, page 18). After 24 hours, seal with acrylic matte varnish. Use artists' acrylic paints to stamp sunflower and leaf motifs onto the door (see Steps 6–8, pages 73–74). Hand-paint highlights on the petals and seeds using bright yellow and burnt sienna artists' acrylic paints; use green to hand-paint the leaves. For the stems, tape lines of low-tack painters' lining tape and paint in. When dry, apply three coats of matte acrylic varnish.
Suitable for all surfaces.

▲ VINEGAR GLAZE AND PLASTIC FILM FROTTAGE

The woody tones of this glaze are combined here with a contemporary gloss finish for a bold, rich style. After priming (see pages 6–9), apply two coats of straw-colored matte latex or wood paint and seal with white shellac. Mix a vinegar glaze to the consistency of milk using burnt sienna and raw umber pigments (see Step 2, page 112). Mask off the outer panel and apply the glaze to the inner panel (see Step 3, page 113). Tear a length of plastic film and lay it over the wet glaze, scrunching it up slightly. Pat it down all over, then pull it back. Remove the tape and repeat, using new plastic film, on the outer panel. When dry, carefully glide on white shellac. After 24 hours, apply three coats of gloss acrylic varnish.
Suitable for wooden and fiberboard surfaces.

▼ MARQUETRY STYLE

Warm tones and a classic inlay design are paired together for a country feel. There is no need to prime the door. Sand the door, then draw out the design in pencil. Use a metal ruler and craft knife to score the design into the wood (see Step 3, page 81). Paint in the design using light oak, dark oak, and red mahogany oil-based wood stains. Allow to dry overnight. Seal with two coats of button polish shellac (or raw umber-tinted white shellac); allow to dry between coats. After 24 hours, apply three coats of semi-gloss acrylic varnish.
Suitable for bare or stripped wooden surfaces such as pine or oak.

▲ TAWNY STIPPLING AND SPONGING

Earthy amber tones create a simple, warming effect. After priming (see pages 6–9), apply two coats of ivory-cream matte latex or wood paint. Mix two acrylic glazes to the consistency of light cream: mix a lighter one using yellow ocher, burnt sienna, and raw umber, and use the same colors, but add more burnt sienna, for a darker one. Mask off the outer panel. Apply the lighter glaze to the inner panel. Stipple (see Liquid glaze effects, page 19) and leave to dry. Dip a damp sea sponge into the darker glaze and dab over the stippled panel, leaving some of the lighter glaze showing through. Soften with a badger-hair softener. Remove the tape from the outer panel and, when dry, mask off the inner panel. Drag the lighter glaze through the outer panel (see Liquid glaze effects, page 19). When dry, apply three coats of matte acrylic varnish.
Suitable for wooden and fiberboard surfaces.

▼ HAND-PAINTED STRIPES

Simple hand-painted stripes produce instant style. After priming (see pages 6–9), apply two coats of pale yellow matte latex or wood paint. Stick down two rows of low-tack painters' tape around the door's edge. Paint freehand stripes using three different shades of yellow paint (see Choosing colors, page 24, for guidance); use three different brushes for varying widths. Don't worry if the stripes wobble—it's all part of the effect. When dry, remove the tape and apply three coats of matte acrylic varnish.
Suitable for all surfaces.

▲ **WHITE-GOLD CHECKS**

After priming (see pages 6–9), apply two coats of cream matte latex or wood paint. Mark a grid of four squares across the width of the inner panel in pencil; seal with white shellac. Cut out transfer metal leaf squares and gild alternate squares (see Steps 4-6, page 117). Apply three coats of button polish shellac (or raw umber-tinted white shellac) to the gilding. Tint metallic varnish yellow; apply three coats to the ungilded squares and door frame.

Suitable for wood and fiberboard surfaces.

▼ **CRAQUELURE ON COPPER LEAF**

Combine copper leaf with craquelure for fiery undertones. After priming (see pages 6–9), apply a coat of deep yellow matte latex or wood paint. Mask off the outer panel and apply white shellac to the inner panel. Gild copper transfer metal leaf to cover the inner panel; seal with white shellac (see Steps 4-7, page 117). When dry, apply both steps of craquelure varnish. After a few hours, rub burnt sienna artists' oil paint into the cracks (see Step 4, page 61). Remove the tape and rub burnt sienna artists' oil paint onto the outer panel. Leave overnight, then seal with button polish shellac (or raw umber-tinted white shellac). When dry, apply three coats of semi-gloss acrylic varnish to the whole door and rub light brown shoe polish onto the outer panel.

Suitable for wooden and fiberboard surfaces.

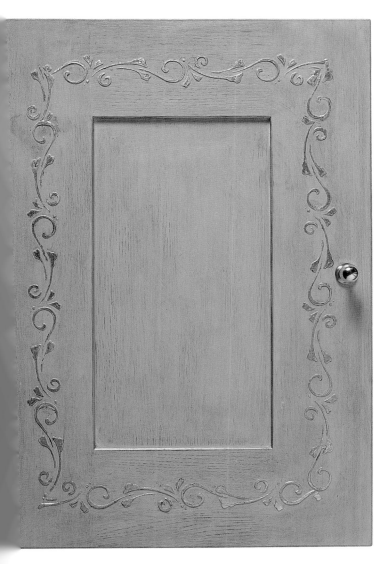

▼ HAND-PAINTED GOLD PANEL

An exquisite hand-painted door in the style of a traditional Japanese screen. After priming (see pages 6–9), apply two coats of light terra cotta matte latex or wood paint. Mask off the outer panel and apply white shellac to the inner panel. Gild Dutch metal transfer leaf to cover the whole panel and seal with white shellac (see Steps 4-7, page 117). Mix a brown and a red paint using artists' acrylic paints and hand-paint brown branches and red blossoms. Remove the tape and rub red wax onto the frame and gilding wax onto the molding (see Colored wax and Gilding wax, page 23). Buff, then varnish the inner panel with two coats of satin polyurethane varnish (see Polyurethane varnish, page 23).

Suitable for wooden and fiberboard surfaces.

▲ GOLD RELIEF STENCILING

The mellow tones of antiqued gold and apricot create a feeling of luxury and warmth. Apply one coat of pale yellow non-absorbent matte latex paint or matte latex paint sealed with matte acrylic varnish and rub back with medium-grade sandpaper to reveal some of the wood. Stencil a linear border with impasto or a thick-textured paint (see Step 3, page 31). When dry, sand any rough edges (see Step 5, page 31). Mix an apricot-colored colorwash and wash over the whole door (see Colorwashing, page 18). When dry, seal the raised stenciling with white shellac. Gild Dutch metal transfer leaf onto the raised areas and seal with white shellac (see Steps 4-7, page 117). When dry, apply three coats of semi-gloss acrylic varnish to the whole door. Rub in dark brown shoe polish and buff.

Suitable for wooden surfaces.

REDS

No matter what the shade, the color red always has a dramatic and immediate impact on a room. It is also one of the best colors for creating a warm, welcoming ambience. Bright reds, berry hues and terra cotta shades lend a lived-in, cozy atmosphere. A versatile color, red is striking, yet subtle when used for broken-color finishes such as color-washing, distressing, and polished plaster effects; it can also be used as a bold note within patterns. Black and cream are both attractive accent colors against a red background. Pale or muted pastel-green shades placed near red will soften the boldness of its impact. The addition of copper and gold metallic effects can be used to enhance the appearance of a warm shade of red; copper will bring out the color's fiery undertones, while gold will create a luxurious, opulent highlight.

Mulberry colorwash & *repeat stamping*

COLORWASH is a popular and widely used technique for creating a beautiful, soft bloom of broken color with far greater depth than plain, flat painting. Equally effective on furniture and walls, it is a simple finish with classic appeal that lends itself to both modern and traditional settings. Above all, it is a relatively quick and easy way to give kitchen doors a facelift at very little cost.

Here we introduce deep, rich berry tones, with a repeat stamp motif in gold, and a brown shadow. The soft beauty of this design in these colors will add a warm and welcoming glow to kitchens large and small.

MATERIALS AND TOOLS

RED NON-ABSORBENT MATTE LATEX PAINT, OR RED
STANDARD MATTE LATEX PAINT
BROWN STENCIL PAINT
GOLD STENCIL PAINT
RED WATER-BASED UNIVERSAL TINTER
MULBERRY COLORWASH
HOUSEHOLD PAINTBRUSH
VARNISH BRUSH
HOG-HAIR SOFTENER
DECORATORS' SPONGE
2 IN (50MM) SPONGE ROLLER
SMALL ROLLER TRAY
METAL RULER
PENCIL
2 SMALL STAMPS ON CLEAR PLASTIC MOUNTING
FINE-GRADE SANDPAPER (FOR A WOODEN DOOR)
MATTE ACRYLIC VARNISH

1 • PREPARATION

Colorwash is ideally suited to solid wood and fiberboard doors, but will also work on melamine, vinyl, or laminate surfaces. Prepare the surface following the instructions on pages 6-9. Use an acrylic or melamine primer, or an acrylic converter (according to door type) and tint with eight to ten drops of red universal tinter, to produce a red-toned primer. Apply a thin, even coat to the door, and allow to dry fully. Apply a second coat. Again, allow to dry fully. Sand between coats on a wooden door only using fine-grade sandpaper.

2 • PAINTING THE BASE COAT

Apply two even coats of red matte latex paint to the door, allowing plenty of time for drying in between. Use a non-absorbent matte latex paint, or, if unavailable, seal a standard matte latex paint with a coat of matte acrylic varnish to make the surface non-absorbent. Sand between coats using fine-grade sandpaper on a wooden door only. Allow a full 24 hours for the paint to cure before applying the colorwash.

5 • VARNISHING

Apply a coat of matte acrylic varnish with a varnish brush, gliding it onto the surface. This seals the colorwash and makes the surface wipeable, a life-saver if you make a mistake during the stamping process. Allow to dry thoroughly. To add extra depth to the color, apply another colorwash following the instructions in steps 3-4; varnish again to seal.

3 • APPLYING THE COLORWASH

Working on one door at a time, pour approximately 1 tbsp (15ml) of mulberry colorwash onto a decorators' sponge. Use the sponge to wipe the colorwash onto the door in swirling figure-of-eight movements, until completely covered. Make sure that there are no gaps in the colorwash.

4 • SOFTENING THE COLORWASH

Immediately take the hog-hair softener and brush softly over the colorwash in light, sweeping crisscross movements, softening and blending the wash. The glaze will quickly become sticky, so you need to work swiftly at this stage. Allow to dry for at least 12 hours.

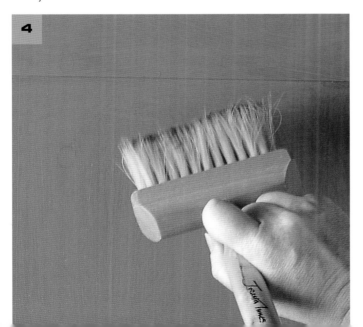

6 • MARKING UP FOR STAMPING

Small repeat motifs are an effective way to introduce a pattern that won't dominate the overall effect. Measure the outer panel of the door and mark the position of the stamping repeats with small pencil dots at regular intervals. Measure and mark the inner panel so that the stamp is repeated between two and three times on each line, creating a diamond repeat pattern. For our design, we used the flower part of the stamp for the outer panel, and both the flower and stem sections of the stamp together for the inner panel.

7 • INKING UP THE STAMP

Pour some brown stencil paint into a small roller tray. Work a 2 in (50mm) sponge roller forwards, backwards, and across the paint until it is evenly distributed on the roller. Roll the paint evenly onto the stamp. Do not overload the stamp, as this will cause the paint to bleed and smudge when you press it onto the surface.

8 • FIRST STAMPING—THE SHADOW

Press the stamp onto the surface, positioning it centrally on one of the pencil dots. Continue inking the stamp and printing in the same way, until you have covered all of the pencil marks. Stamp the inner panel first, starting at the top left-hand corner if you are right-handed, or at the top right-hand corner if you are left-handed, to avoid smudging. Then stamp the pattern onto the outer panel. Allow to dry thoroughly.

9 • SECOND STAMPING—THE HIGHLIGHT

Clean and dry the roller and stamp. Ink up the stamp with gold stencil paint. To highlight the shadow below, place the stamp slightly to the right of the brown stamped motif already created—the clear plastic mounting of the stamp will make a good registration guide. Repeat over all of the previous stamping, and leave the paint to dry thoroughly.

10 • FINISHING

Varnish the door with two coats of matte acrylic varnish, allowing the first coat to dry thoroughly before applying the second.

HARDWARE

Burnished or antiqued brass or gold-effect knobs or handles will reflect the highlights and warm, rich hues of this design.

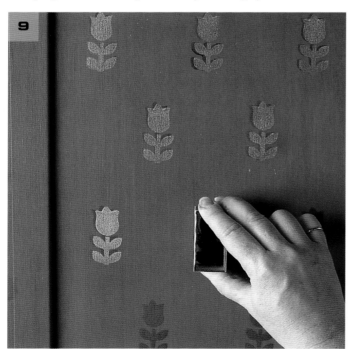

TRADE SECRETS

- *When painting a melamine or vinyl surface, be sure to leave adequate drying time between coats. Doing so will enhance the bonding process, making the finish more durable.*

- *The stamp must be pressed firmly down perpendicular to the surface, or the edges of the image may turn out fuzzy. The best way to ensure a straight image is to stand directly behind the stamp, not to the side of it—this will help you line it up with maximum accuracy.*

Terra cotta polished plaster
& copper squares

POLISHED PLASTER CREATES a classical finish for both traditional and contemporary interiors, adding a lustrous depth and sheen that is hard to achieve with paint alone. Also known as marmorino, stucco, Venetian plaster, Swedish putty, or brushing putty, polished plaster contains marble dust, making it possible to create the look of real, polished marble; the resulting effect is sumptuous, highly distinctive elegance. Although it takes a bit of practice and time to apply, the results of this finish are truly rewarding.

Here we work with polished plaster which has been tinted to a rich terra cotta color. The plaster is then given extra sheen with a ruby-colored wax, and copper highlights are added for a contemporary twist.

1 • PREPARATION
This technique is only suitable for solid wood or fiberboard doors—it will not work on melamine, vinyl, or laminate surfaces. Sand the door using fine-grade sandpaper, then seal it with slightly diluted water-based white glue. Apply an even coat of acrylic primer. When dry, sand down any ridges.

2 • TINTING THE PLASTER
You will need about 6 tbsp (90ml) of polished plaster for an average-sized cupboard door. Put the plaster into a plastic paint pail, add four to five drops each of red and burnt sienna water-based universal tinters, and stir thoroughly, until all of the color has been mixed in.

MATERIALS AND TOOLS
ACRYLIC PRIMER
POLISHED PLASTER
UNIVERSAL TINTERS: RED, BURNT SIENNA
FITCH BRUSH
HOUSEHOLD PAINTBRUSH
ARTISTS' SABLE BRUSH
DECORATORS' STEEL FLOAT
COPPER TRANSFER METAL LEAF
ACRYLIC GILDING SIZE
PAINT PAIL
METAL RULER
PENCIL
SHARP SCISSORS
CARDBOARD
LINT-FREE CLOTH
WATER-BASED WHITE GLUE
FINE-GRADE SANDPAPER
CLEAR BEESWAX POLISH
RED-TINTED WAX POLISH
WHITE SHELLAC

TRADE SECRETS

• *Plaster may crack if applied too thickly. Practice the technique on a piece of board before applying it to a door.*

• *A wax finish is not suitable around sinks or areas that may get wet. As an alternative, apply one coat of gloss acrylic varnish tinted with one to two drops of red water-based universal tinter. Brush on evenly, working around the copper squares. Apply a second coat of clear, untinted gloss varnish over the entire surface of the door, including the squares.*

3 • APPLYING THE FIRST LAYER

Spoon 3 tbsp (45ml) of polished plaster onto the top edge of a decorators' steel float, and smooth it onto the entire surface of the door in wide, arcing movements. Make sure that the entire surface is covered evenly with the plaster, which should be about $\frac{1}{8}$ in (3mm) thick, and that no plaster is wrapped around the sides. After making the surface as smooth as possible, leave for 10-15 minutes, then return and smooth again with the edge of the float, removing any excess plaster or ridges. Allow to dry a little more, then smooth over once again.

4 • APPLYING THE SECOND LAYER

When the first layer of plaster is almost dry (it will be cold to the touch), apply a second coat, about $\frac{1}{8}$ in (3mm) thick, as before. Leave for about 10 minutes, then return and smooth over. Return thereafter at 5-10 minute intervals and smooth, applying a firmer pressure to the float each time. With each successive smoothing process, a natural sheen will begin to appear. The more effort put in at this stage, the higher the luster. Allow to dry completely for 24 hours.

5 • MARKING UP

Use a ruler and a pencil to mark up 1 in (25mm) squares on the back of the copper transfer sheets, then cut out with a pair of sharp scissors. You will need about ten squares per door. Cut out a 4 in (100mm) cardboard square to use as a template. Turn the cardboard onto the diagonal, and position it so that it can fit into the width of your door roughly twice (if it fits in more than twice, increase the size of your template accordingly). Starting about $1\frac{1}{2}$ in (40mm) from the top of the door, draw pencil marks at the corners of the cardboard. Mark up the entire door in this way. Draw a 1 in (25mm) square around each dot, centering it.

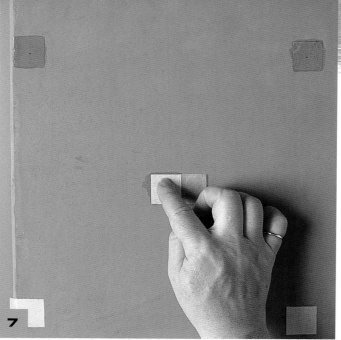

6 • APPLYING GILDING SIZE

Using a fitch brush, apply a small amount of white shellac to each square to seal that area of the plaster. Allow to dry thoroughly, then use an artists' sable brush to add a fine, even layer of acrylic gilding size to each square. Leave for about 15 minutes, or until the size becomes translucent.

7 • APPLYING THE COPPER LEAF

Carefully press the copper leaf squares onto the sized squares, rubbing the transfer backing paper carefully with your finger to ensure the copper adheres fully. Carefully peel away the transfer backing paper. Seal each square with a small amount of white shellac, and leave until completely dry.

HARDWARE

A terra cotta knob with a copper square detail is the ideal match for this design. If drilling the knob in, affix masking tape to the door's surface and carefully drill through to prevent the plaster from cracking.

8 • FINISHING

Using a lint-free cloth, apply clear beeswax polish to the door, carefully working around the copper squares. The polish will be readily absorbed into the porous surface of the plaster. Gently remove the excess wax, then buff. Apply a thin coat of red-tinted wax polish, again avoiding the copper squares. Remove any excess wax, then buff up to a full sheen. Any effort put into polishing at this stage will be significant— the more you buff, the deeper the sheen.

Limed finish
on *marquetry-style wood paint*

LIMING ADDS a beautiful silvery bloom to open-grained hardwoods such as oak and ash, and softens and lightens the look of woods that otherwise may appear heavy or drab. The limed look has a timeless appeal, and brings classic distinction to any kitchen.

Here we use a modern liming paste—which doesn't have the caustic properties of traditional slaked lime. Because liming paste can be varnished, it is especially appropriate for the kitchen. A colored marquetry-style design has been added before liming the doors for an exceptionally stylish and unique overall look.

MATERIALS AND TOOLS
WATER-BASED HIGHLY PIGMENTED WOOD PAINT OR ACRYLIC WOOD STAINS: RED, ORANGE, YELLOW
STIFF WIRE BRUSH
HOUSEHOLD PAINTBRUSH
2 VARNISH BRUSHES
½ IN (13MM) ONE-STROKE BRUSH, SABLE OR NYLON
ARTISTS' SABLE BRUSH
DUSTING BRUSH
SMALL SOFT WIRE BRUSH—AS USED ON SUEDE
PAINT STRIPPER
LIMING PASTE
2 DAMP CLOTHS
METAL RULER
PENCIL
SHARP CRAFT KNIFE
DUST MASK
FINE-GRADE SANDPAPER
WHITE SHELLAC
MATTE ACRYLIC VARNISH

1 • PREPARATION
This technique is only suitable for hardwood doors with an open grain—it will not work on melamine, vinyl, or laminate surfaces, nor on soft woods, such as pine. Older wood must be stripped and sanded down (see pages 8-9). Do not prime the doors.

2 • ENHANCING THE GRAIN
Use a stiff wire brush to "rake" out the grain, brushing firmly and always working in the direction of the grain. Brush off, then wipe with a damp cloth to remove all loose matter.

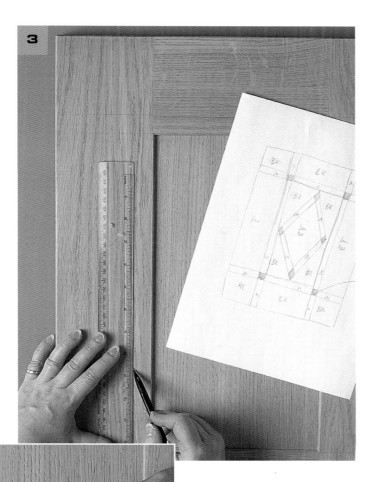

4 • PAINTING THE DESIGN

Dilute three water-based wood paint colors, using three parts water to two parts wood paint, or use acrylic wood stain colors. We used a rich berry red, guava orange, and warm yellow. Paint the wood paint or stain onto the door as evenly as possible, brushing in the direction of the grain. Use a ½ in (13mm) one-stroke brush for large areas, and an artists' sable brush for fine lines and edges. Allow to dry fully.

5 • APPLYING THE LIMING PASTE

Stir the liming paste well before use. With a household paintbrush, apply a thick, even coat of paste over the door, painting in the direction of the grain. The paste will mask the design beneath, but don't worry, it will be revealed again later. Leave the paste to dry for one hour, or until completely dry.

3 • DRAWING AND SCORING THE DESIGN

Choose a simple geometric design for your door based on diamonds or squares. Make a rough plan of the design first, then transfer it to the door using a ruler and a pencil. Keep the pencil lines light, so that they will not be visible later. Using a ruler and a craft knife, lightly score along the pencil lines. The scored lines will help you achieve crisp edges when applying the paint or stain.

6

6 • REMOVING THE LIMING PASTE

Wear a dust mask at this stage, to avoid inhaling any dust. Using a small soft wire brush, gently brush away the paste, working in the direction of the grain. Brush the excess dust off with a dusting brush, or vacuum it away, then go back over it with a slightly damp cloth to remove all remaining dust.

7 • SEALING

The marquetry-style design will now have a beautiful pastel-like, silvery appearance. Use a varnish brush to carefully apply an even coat of white shellac to the entire door, taking care not to dislodge the liming paste in the grain.

8 • FINISHING

Varnish with three coats of matte acrylic varnish, allowing each coat to dry thoroughly before applying the next.

7

HARDWARE

A wooden knob painted and limed to match the door lends a sense of continuity to this soft, rich effect.

Shades of scarlet

Here we see how reds can be used to create a wide range of effects, each with its own unique ambience. From the beauty of wood graining in rich cherry tones to funky colorwashed checks in red and orange, and from a luxurious red-and-black tortoiseshell design to simple Chinese red lacquer-style, it is possible to achieve a sense of drama, cheerfulness, or elegance with the red palette.

▲ FANTASY WOOD GRAIN

A faux wood grain that imitates burr walnut. After priming (see pages 6–9), apply two coats of light terra cotta matte latex or wood paint and seal with white shellac. Mix up a chestnut-brown vinegar glaze to the consistency of milk using burnt sienna and burnt umber pigments (see Step 2, page 112). Brush the glaze onto the inner panel (see Step 3, page 113), then roll a sausage-shaped piece of plasticine over it to create a regular pattern. Dab a damp sea sponge over the pattern to reveal some base color; soften with a badger-hair softener. Repeat on the outer panel. When dry, carefully glide on a coat of button polish shellac (or raw umber-tinted white shellac). Do not brush over any area twice. When dry, shellac again, then apply three coats of semi-gloss acrylic varnish. *Suitable for all surfaces.*

◀ FRUIT DECOUPAGE

A fruit decoupage design makes a classic, stylish statement. After priming (see pages 6–9), apply two coats of cream matte latex or wood paint. Seal fruit decoupage motifs with button polish shellac (or raw umber-tinted white shellac); cut out when dry. Stick each motif onto the inner panel using diluted water-based white glue (see Step 5, page 39). Seal with white shellac. Paint bright red matte latex on the inside rim of the panel and on the outer edges of the door. When dry, varnish with two coats of matte acrylic varnish tinted with two drops of raw umber. *Suitable for all surfaces.*

▲ CHERRY STENCIL ON SPATTER

A simple fruit stencil on a subtle veil of spattered color produces this lively effect. After priming (see pages 6–9), apply two coats of coffee-cream matte latex or wood paint. Mask off the outer panel. Mix up a light terra cotta glaze to the consistency of milk (see Liquid glaze effects, page 19) and brush onto the inner panel; stipple (see Liquid glaze effects, page 19). Add 2 tsp (10ml) of water and two drops of burnt sienna and yellow ocher universal tinters to the glaze and spatter the inner panel (see Step 6, page 95). Add two more drops of burnt sienna and three drops of red and spatter again. Finally, spatter with diluted coffee-cream paint. Use a simple fruit motif and stencil with red and green stencil paint. Hand-paint dark green veins onto the leaves. Paint the inner rim of the inside panel red. Remove the tape. Leave to dry overnight, then apply three coats of matte acrylic varnish. *Suitable for all surfaces.*

▼ RED COLORWASH CHECK

Red and orange checks make a bold, funky statement. After priming (see pages 6–9), apply two coats of matte cream-colored non-absorbent latex paint or matte latex paint sealed with matte acrylic varnish. Stick horizontal rows of low-tack painters' tape at 4 in (100mm) and 1 in (25mm) intervals. Mix a red colorwash and wash over the door; soften with a hog-hair softener (see Colorwashing, page 18). With a slightly damp sea sponge, wipe away the colorwash from the narrow stripes. When dry, drag a bright yellow colorwash over the narrow stripes (see Liquid glaze effects, page 19). When dry, stick vertical rows of low-tack painters' tape at the same intervals and repeat the colorwashing process. Remove the tape. After 24 hours, apply three coats of semi-gloss acrylic varnish. *Suitable for all surfaces; man-made surfaces will require more drying time.*

▼ RED·BLACK TORTOISESHELL

Faux tortoiseshell creates a traditional Victorian look. After priming (see pages 6–9), apply two coats of red matte latex or wood paint. When dry, mask off the frame and brush acrylic glazing liquid (the consistency of thick cream) onto the panels (see Liquid glaze effects, page 19). Mix three parts burnt sienna to one part black artists' acrylic paints together and hand-paint diagonal oblong shapes. Add black to the mixture and paint dark lines around the shapes. Dab a damp sea sponge over the marks to reveal the base color; soften with a badger-hair softener. Mix two drops of crimson and burnt sienna tinters in button polish shellac (or raw umber-tinted white shellac) and apply two coats (allow to dry between coats). Remove the tape; apply three coats of semi-gloss acrylic varnish. Apply gold gilding wax (see Gilding wax, page 23) or gold varnish to the molding.

Suitable for all surfaces; most effective on small panels.

▲ MAHOGANY GRAINING AND TROMPE L'OEIL MOLDING

This faux wood grain effect emulates rich mahogany paneling. After priming (see pages 6–9), apply a coat of terra cotta satin latex paint. Mask off a frame of low-tack painters' tape 3 in (70mm) in from the door's edge. Mix a glaze to the consistency of light cream and color with burnt umber and a drop of black artists' acrylics. Brush the glaze over the whole door, then hand-paint random stripes and a mahogany grain pattern using burnt umber and black. Flog (see Step 3, page 57); soften with a badger-hair softener. When dry, remove the tape and mask the painted areas around the unpainted lines. Drag a nearly-black glaze over the unpainted stripes (see Liquid glaze effects, page 19). When dry, re-tape and paint a brown line down the center of each stripe. Remove the tape. Seal with button polish shellac (or raw umber-tinted white shellac). When dry, varnish with three coats of semi-gloss acrylic varnish.

Suitable for all surfaces; most effective on a flat door.

▼ BRIGHT LACQUER

The glossy effect of traditional lacquer is recreated in a contemporary style. Apply two coats of primer tinted red (see pages 6–9), sanding between coats, then apply two coats of bright red matte latex or wood paint; sand between coats once again. When dry, apply white shellac as smoothly as possible. After 24 hours, apply a second coat. More coats of shellac can be added for a deeper luster and sheen if desired. Always allow the shellac to dry for 24 hours between coats. Apply three coats of gloss acrylic varnish.

Suitable for all surfaces; most effective on a flat or Shaker-style door.

▲ HAND-PAINTED STRIPES AND DISTRESSED PAINTWORK

This technique creates a fun, contemporary feel—try it in bold shades, or in muted, subtle tones (see Choosing colors, pages 24-27, for guidance). After priming (see pages 6–9), apply two coats of cream matte latex or wood paint. Mask off the outer panel and select five shades of wood paint. Starting on the left, hand-paint stripes down the length of the panel using a ¼ in (5mm) one-stroke brush. Repeat the colors in the same order across the panel. Go over stripes twice to ensure coverage. When dry, apply a coat of matte acrylic varnish. Remove the tape and mask off the inner panel. Rub candle wax onto the frame, then paint the frame and inside rim with two coats of red matte latex paint; when dry, distress with medium-grade steel wool (see Distressing, page 18). Varnish with three coats of matte acrylic varnish.

Suitable for wooden surfaces.

BLUES & GREENS

RELAXING, HARMONIOUS, AND PEACEFUL ARE WORDS THAT ARE COMMONLY USED TO DESCRIBE THE BLUE AND GREEN PALETTE. TYPICALLY ASSOCIATED WITH THE NATURAL WORLD, BLUES AND GREENS REMIND US OF BLUE SKIES, SPRING LEAVES, RIVERS, AND OCEANS—THE PLACES WE VISIT TO UNWIND AND RELAX. ON ITS OWN, BLUE IS A CONTEMPLATIVE, RESTFUL COLOR, WHILE GREEN IS SOMEWHAT MORE VIGOROUS, YET REGENERATIVE AND BALANCED. WHEN PAIRED TOGETHER, THE RESULT IS AN AMBIENCE THAT IS RESTFUL, SOOTHING, AND HARMONIOUS. BOTH COLORS LEND THEMSELVES TO A WIDE VARIETY OF FINISHES, AND ARE INHERENTLY WELL SUITED TO TRADITIONAL AS WELL AS CONTEMPORARY STYLES. AS RECEDING COLORS, BLUES AND GREENS ARE OFTEN USED AS PART OF A PATTERN, USUALLY IN COMBINATION WITH WHITE; THEY ARE ALSO EFFECTIVE WHEN USED ALONE, AS PLAIN, FLAT COLORS. IN ROOMS WHERE COOLER SHADES OF BLUE OR GREEN FEATURE PROMINENTLY, ACCENTS OF RED, ORANGE, OR YELLOW CAN BE ADDED FOR A SENSE OF WARMTH.

Gingham *checks*

USING GLAZING LIQUID EFFECTS to emulate different types of textiles and textures is a popular and fashionable design source for interiors. Here we pick up on this trend, using glazing liquid to create a wonderful gingham texture. Ideal for adding charm and character to cottage- or Shaker-style kitchens, this paint finish can be used throughout your kitchen, or on occasional units only—paint the remaining units in the same two shades used to make the checks. Based on dragging using a specialist long-bristled brush, the actual paint technique used to create this finish is very simple. All you need is a little time and patience—and plenty of lining tape!

MATERIALS AND TOOLS
WATER-BASED UNIVERSAL TINTERS: GREEN, RAW UMBER
IVORY HIGHLY PIGMENTED WOOD PAINT
2 HOUSEHOLD PAINTBRUSHES
2 VARNISH BRUSHES, ONE IN A SMALLER SIZE
SMALL DRAGGING BRUSH
ARTISTS' SABLE BRUSH
⅜ IN (10MM) LOW-TACK LINING TAPE
METAL RULER
PENCIL
CARPENTERS' SQUARE OR SPIRIT LEVEL
PLASTIC OR GUM ERASER
PAINT PAIL
FINE-GRADE SANDPAPER
ACRYLIC GLAZING LIQUID
SEMI-GLOSS ACRYLIC VARNISH

1 • PREPARATION
Prepare a solid wood or fiberboard surface following instructions on pages 6-9. Apply two coats of ivory wood paint, sanding between coats using fine-grade sandpaper. When dry, apply a coat of semi-gloss acrylic varnish with a varnish brush. Allow to dry fully.

2 • TAPING THE FIRST LINES
Use low-tack lining tape to mask the molding between the inner and outer panels. Start applying the tape in vertical lines on the inner panel. The gap between lines should be the same thickness as the tape—use a ruler for complete accuracy. Draw a line around the center of the outer panel; fix the tape centrally over the line.

3 • MIXING THE GLAZE
Pour two parts acrylic glazing liquid into a paint pail, and make up the final third with equal parts of water and eggshell acrylic varnish. Add four or five drops of green water-based universal tinter, then tone down slightly with a drop of raw umber. Stir well.

4 • DRAGGING THE GLAZE

Using a small varnish brush, brush the glaze onto the inner panel of the door, making sure that an even coverage is achieved. Take a small dragging brush and drag it down the door through the glaze, repeating this movement until you have achieved an even set of dragged lines through the still-wet glaze. Glaze and drag the outer panel of the door as well, brushing downward on the vertical and across on the horizontal. Allow to dry for 30 minutes.

5 • REMOVING THE TAPE

When the glaze begins to harden, peel off all of the tape lines, with the exception of those masking the molding (this will be left ivory). Allow to dry for two full hours, or until the glaze has hardened.

6 • TAPING THE SECOND LINES

Fix lines of tape at right angles to the first lines—use a carpenters' square or spirit level for guidance if you like. Once again, the gap between the lines should be the same thickness as the tape. Place a piece of tape continuing the line of the molding at each end of the door frame, creating a right-angle square in each corner. Make a smaller right angle at the corner, lining the tape up with the previous line. The corner lines should now show two right angles (see above inset).

TRADE SECRETS

- *The best way to achieve an even coverage of glaze when dragging is to apply the glaze sparingly.*

- *The lines of tape should be removed as soon as the glaze starts hardening, but before it dries completely. If they are left until the glaze has hardened fully, removing them will be difficult, and the surface below may become damaged in the process.*

7 • DRAGGING THE SECOND GLAZE

Apply an even coat of glaze onto the inner panel with the smaller varnish brush. Take the small dragging brush and drag it horizontally across the door—if the door is off its hinges, turn it so that you can drag in a downward motion—until you have evenly dragged lines. Leave the glaze to dry until it starts to harden, then remove the tape, including those strips covering the molding.

8 • PAINTING IN DETAIL

To create an effective gingham-style border, take up some of the glaze on an artists' sable brush, and paint small strokes imitating a backstitch down the center of the ivory line left on the outer panel. Allow to dry for 24 hours, or until fully dry.

HARDWARE

A plain white ceramic or enamel knob or a simple chrome handle would be a perfect finishing touch for this charming design.

9 • FINISHING

Erase the pencil lines on the outer panel and brush or vacuum away the eraser dust. Apply three coats of semi-gloss acrylic varnish, allowing each coat to dry thoroughly before applying the next.

Duck-egg *speckle*

2

BASED ON THE ESTABLISHED paint technique of spattering, the subtle veil of speckled color created by this effect is often used to imitate the look of natural stones and precious minerals such as sandstone, porphyry, granite, and lapis lazuli. Here we use this technique to produce a slightly different, more delicate effect, recreating the look of a duck-egg shell in blues and grays.

A very simple technique, spattering relies upon the subtlety of similar tones and hues spattered finely onto a pale, stippled background. Ideally applied to plain, flat cupboard doors or large paneled doors, this effect is perfect for a room that needs a slight lift, but not necessarily a radical transformation.

MATERIALS AND TOOLS
Pale blue matte latex paint
Artists' acrylic paints: green, blue, black, raw umber, white
2 household paintbrushes
Varnish brush
5 fitch brushes or stencil brushes
Paint pail
Low-tack painters' tape
Stippling block
Paint mixing palette or saucers
Step ladder (optional)
Fine-grade sandpaper (for a wooden door)
Acrylic glazing liquid
Matte acrylic varnish

1 • PREPARATION
Prepare a solid wood, fiber-board, melamine, vinyl, or laminate surface following the instructions on pages 6-9, laying on two coats of primer. Apply two coats of pale blue matte latex paint, allowing the first coat to dry thoroughly before applying the second. Sand between coats using fine-grade sandpaper on a wooden door only. Allow a full 24 hours for the paint to dry. Using a varnish brush, apply a coat of matte acrylic varnish, and allow to dry thoroughly.

2 • MIXING THE GLAZE
Make up a glaze in a paint pail as follows: add a bit of blue and green artists' acrylic paint to a mixture of two-thirds acrylic glazing liquid to one-third equal amounts of matte acrylic varnish and water. (The varnish is used here to hasten the drying time of the glaze).

3

3 • MASKING THE PANEL
Using low-tack painters' tape, mask off the entire outer panel, leaving the inner panel clear.

4 • STIPPLING THE GLAZE

Using a household paintbrush, apply a coat of glaze to the door panel in uneven, loose brushstrokes. Take the stippling block and, using a "pouncing" motion, work it into the still-wet glaze. Continue stippling, wiping any excess glaze off the block as you work, until a soft veil of glaze covers the entire panel. Set aside for approximately 30 minutes, or until the glaze starts to harden.

5 • MIXING COLORS FOR SPATTERING

Make five different colors as follows: create an off-white by mixing a dab of raw umber with white; a pale turquoise using white, and a bit of blue and green; a mid-tone turquoise using white, more blue, and a dab of green; a mid-tone gray using white, black, and a dab of raw umber; and a darker gray using white, more black, and a dab of raw umber. Add water to each of the colors, until all are the consistency of light cream.

6 • SPATTERING

Spatter using each of the five colors, as follows: dip a dry fitch or stencil brush into the paint, and position it directly in front of the area to be spattered. If you have not removed the door, and it is above you, use a step ladder to position yourself level with the surface to be spattered, to avoid dribbles. Holding the brush in one hand, flick it down over the forefinger of your other hand. Spatter first with the pale turquoise, covering the entire area with a fine spray. Next, spatter the darker turquoise, then the mid-tone gray, then the dark gray, and finally, the white. Allow to dry for a full 24 hours.

7 • REMOVING THE TAPE
When the spattered paint has fully dried, remove the painters' tape by gently peeling it back upon itself.

TRADE SECRETS

- *For this technique to work properly, it is important that the paint be the right density. If the paint drips before you begin spattering, this means that it is too thin; if the paint comes off the brush in large droplets during spattering, dilute it with water.*

- *It is best to remove the door so that you can spatter while standing above it, ensuring an even distribution of spatter marks. If removal is impossible, use a step ladder to position yourself level with the surface while spattering. This will help prevent the spattered paint from becoming overly dense at the bottom.*

8 • FINISHING
When the paint is completely dry, apply three coats of matte acrylic varnish, allowing each coat to dry thoroughly before applying the next.

HARDWARE
Brushed silver handles are the natural choice to illuminate the cool blue tones of this design.

Blue-and-white
Portuguese-style folk art

Blue and white is a popular color combination, and is often prominent in crockery and ceramics. The famous Willow pattern, based on Oriental chinoiserie designs, Delft tiles and ceramics from Holland, Spode china, and traditional Mediterranean pottery have all made use of this attractive pairing of colors.

Here we apply the crisp simplicity of blue and white to the kitchen, developing a design based upon an original piece of Portuguese pottery painted in a folk art style.

MATERIALS AND TOOLS

WHITE MATTE LATEX PAINT
ARTISTS' ACRYLIC PAINTS: COBALT BLUE,
ULTRAMARINE BLUE, WHITE
HOUSEHOLD PAINTBRUSH
VARNISH BRUSH
MEDIUM ARTISTS' SABLE BRUSH
FINE ARTISTS' SABLE BRUSH
SHARP PENCIL
TRANSFER PAPER
LOW-TACK PAINTERS' TAPE
2 JAM JARS
LINT-FREE CLOTH
FINE-GRADE SANDPAPER (FOR A WOODEN DOOR)
ACRYLIC GLAZING LIQUID
MATTE ACRYLIC VARNISH
BLUE-TINTED WAX POLISH

1 • PREPARATION

This technique lends itself to solid wood doors with central panels, but it can also be applied to melamine, laminate, vinyl, and fiberboard doors. Prepare the surface following the instructions on pages 6-9. Apply two coats of white matte latex paint, allowing the first coat to dry before applying the second. Sand between coats using fine-grade sandpaper on a wooden door only. With a varnish brush, apply one coat of matte acrylic varnish.

2 • TRACING THE DESIGN

Choose a blue-and-white ceramic design. On a piece of transfer paper, trace the main part of the design—our chosen design's main section shows a collection of flowers and leaves. If the design needs to be elongated in order to fit the central panel, parts of it can be repeated.

3

4

3 • TRANSFERRING THE DESIGN

Turn the transfer paper over and center it on the door panel, holding it in place with some masking tape. Using a sharp pencil, draw over each traced line, transferring the design onto the door.

4 • DESIGNING THE BORDER

Select a detail from the original design that can be repeated as a border. Trace and transfer this design as before, around the border of the door. Alternatively, draw a border freehand, or paint a simple thin line using two lines of low-tack painters' tape as a guide.

5 • MIXING THE PAINT

Mix some cobalt blue and ultramarine blue artists' acrylic paint together in two separate jam jars. Add different amounts of white artists' acrylic paint to each jar, creating a mid-tone blue and a darker shade of blue. Add a little acrylic glazing liquid and water to both mixtures until they are the consistency of light cream.

6

6 • PAINTING THE DESIGN

Using a medium artists' sable brush, paint in the design with the mid-toned blue; use the original design as a guide. Paint using short, rounded, brushstrokes for a folk art look. When dry, take up some dark blue on the fine artists' sable brush and paint in the shadows and details. Paint the border pattern in the same way.

7 • ADDING DECORATIVE DETAIL

Take up some of the dark blue on the fine sable brush and hold the loaded paintbrush at a slight angle to the edge of the raised panel or molding. Run the brush along the molding to create a thin line. Mix a pale wash by adding more water to the mid-tone blue paint, then use the medium artists' sable brush to paint this wash along the molding. Allow to dry thoroughly.

8 • FINISHING

Apply three coats of matte acrylic varnish, allowing each coat to dry thoroughly before applying the next. Take up some blue-tinted wax polish on a lint-free cloth and apply it to the edges and corners of the panel and border to create areas of soft shading.

HARDWARE

Paint a wooden knob using white wood paint, and allow to dry thoroughly. Choose a detail from your design, and copy it onto the knob using either the mid-tone or darker blue—or both—as you like.

TRADE SECRETS

- *Use loose brushstrokes to paint in the less intricate parts of the design, holding the brush handle anywhere from the middle to the tip for greater ease of movement. This will result in a "folk art" painting style. For the more detailed portions of the design, hold the brush handle closer to the bristles to achieve greater control.*

Ocean splendor

Blues and greens in both deep and pastel shades lend themselves to modern styles, as well as to more traditional ones—designs that combine both styles suit this palette as well. Delicate hand-painted willow leaves in muted greens, a faux lapis lazuli finish, stylish polished plaster squares in aqua hues, and distressing in rich blue and pale green are just a few examples of how this color palette can be used to gorgeous effect.

▲ HAND-PAINTED WILLOW

A delicate willow design in muted greens creates a sense of calm. Prime (see pages 6–9), then apply two coats of pale green non-absorbent matte latex paint or matte latex paint sealed with matte acrylic varnish. Mix a pale green colorwash (see Colorwashing, page 18) and wash over the door. Leave overnight, then seal with matte acrylic varnish. Transfer a willow design to the door (see Step 6, page 36). Paint the leaves using two tones of green and the twigs using brown. Mask a border with low-tack painters' tape; paint in green to the near edges of the willow design (see photo). Remove the tape. Apply three coats of matte acrylic varnish.

Suitable for all surfaces.

◀ DISTRESSING, STENCILING, AND WAXING

A charming Provençal-style design. After priming (see pages 6–9), apply two coats of blue matte latex or wood paint. Rub on some candle wax. Apply two coats of pale green matte latex wood paint. When dry, distress with medium-grade steel wool (see Distressing, page 18). Using a linear stencil and a slightly darker green, stencil the upright panels. When dry, apply three coats of matte acrylic varnish. Highlight the molding and stenciling with gold gilding wax (see Gilding wax, page 23).

Suitable for all surfaces.

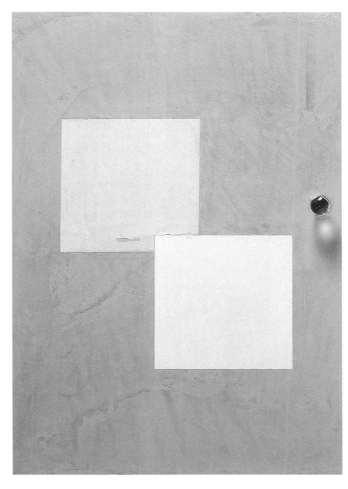

▼ DISTRESSED PAINT AND EMBROIDERY SAMPLER EFFECT

An embroidery sampler is set off against distressed paintwork for a folksy look. After priming (see pages 6–9), apply two coats of pale gray matte latex or wood paint. Rub on some candle wax, then paint with two coats of pale green matte latex or wood paint. When dry, distress with medium-grade steel wool (see Distressing, page 18). Seal a color photocopy of an embroidery sampler with white shellac (see Step 2, page 38); when dry, cut to fit the door panel. Stick this down using diluted water-based white glue, laying the top down first, then smoothing the whole picture down. When dry, seal with white shellac. Allow to dry completely, then apply three coats of matte acrylic varnish.

Suitable for wooden and fiberboard surfaces.

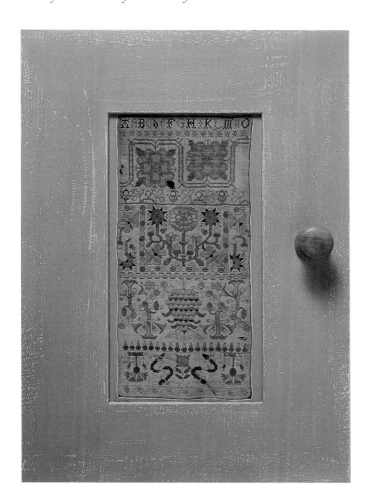

▲ POLISHED PLASTER SQUARES

A stylish, modern design using polished plaster in three tones. Apply two coats of primer tinted green (see pages 6–9). Mix up aquamarine, white, and pale aqua (aquamarine mixed with the white) batches of polished plaster (see Step 2, page 76). Apply a fine layer of the aquamarine, remove the excess, and smooth out (see Step 3, page 77). When dry, apply a second coat; when nearly dry, polish to a sheen (see Step 4, page 77). Mark up two overlapping squares. Stick low-tack painters' tape around the lower square. Apply two thin coats of pale aqua plaster to the masked square and polish. When dry, remove the tape. Tape up the overlapping square and repeat the process with the white plaster. Polish the entire surface when dry. Seal with gloss acrylic varnish or liquid wax (see Liquid waxes, page 23).

Suitable for flat wooden and fiberboard surfaces.

▼ HAND-PAINTED STRIPES

Cool blue and green stripes make a bold statement. After priming (see pages 6–9), apply two coats of pale turquoise matte latex or wood paint. When dry, affix two rows of low-tack painters' tape around the door's frame. Select four shades of blue and green matte latex or wood paint (see Choosing colors, pages 24-27, for guidance). Paint freehand stripes using different brushes to create different stripe widths. Don't worry if the stripes wobble—it's part of the look. When dry, remove the tapes. Apply three coats of semi-gloss acrylic varnish. *Suitable for all surfaces.*

▲ BLUE COLORWASH WITH GOLD STENCIL

Rich blue with sophisticated gold stenciling adds a splash of color to the kitchen. After priming (see pages 6–9), apply two coats of matte pale turquoise non-absorbent latex paint or matte latex paint sealed with matte acrylic varnish. Mix a cobalt blue colorwash and wash over the door (see Colorwashing, page 18). After 24 hours, seal with matte acrylic varnish. Apply a second coat of colorwash to the central panel. Stencil gold stencil paint through a linear border stencil on the vertical outer panels. Leave for 24 hours, then varnish with three coats of matte or semi-gloss acrylic varnish. *Suitable for all surfaces.*

▼ LAPIS LAZULI EFFECT

Lapis lazuli with gold distressing creates a sumptuous feel. Prime, (see pages 6–9) then apply two coats of turquoise matte latex or wood paint (sand between coats). Mix an ultramarine glaze and a Prussian blue glaze (see Liquid glaze effects, page 19) to the consistency of light cream. Mask off the outer panel. Using two sea sponges, dab both colors onto the inner panel, leaving some base color showing through. Leave for 10 minutes and repeat; repeat a third time. Paint tiny dots of gilding size randomly across the surface; dab on gold metallic powder. After 10 minutes, brush off the excess. Seal the gold dots with white shellac. When dry, remove the tape from the frame, rub on candle wax, and cover with gold paint. Distress with medium-grade steel wool (see Distressing, page 18) when dry. Apply three coats of semi-gloss acrylic varnish. *Suitable for wooden and fiberboard surfaces.*

▲ WOVEN DENIM EFFECT

The simple appeal of denim is used here to stylish effect. After priming (see pages 6–9), mask off the outer panel. Apply two coats of pale blue matte latex or wood paint to the inner panel. Seal with matte acrylic varnish. Mix up a glaze using $\frac{2}{3}$ matte acrylic varnish and $\frac{1}{3}$ water to the consistency of light cream and tint with blue, raw umber, and a little white (see Liquid glaze effects, page 19). Brush the glaze vertically and evenly onto the inner panel, then drag a dragging brush repeatedly through the glaze until an even effect is achieved (see Dragging, page 19). After 15 minutes, repeat the dragging process horizontally. When dry, varnish with matte acrylic varnish. Mask off the inner panel. Paint the outer panel and edges with two coats of sea blue-colored matte latex or wood paint. When dry, apply three coats of matte acrylic varnish. *Suitable for all door surfaces.*

BLACK, WHITE & GRAY

WHETHER USED ALONE OR IN COMBINATION, BLACK, WHITE, AND GRAY ARE TYPICALLY ASSOCIATED WITH A SLEEK, MODERN STYLE. BLACK ON ITS OWN SHOULD BE USED SPARINGLY, AS IT ABSORBS LIGHT. FOR A REFLECTIVE QUALITY, A BLACK SURFACE CAN BE FINISHED WITH GLOSS OR METALLIC VARNISH. BLACK CAN ALSO BE LIGHTENED TO A CHARCOAL SHADE FOR A SOFTER, MORE SUBTLE EFFECT. WHEN PAIRED WITH WHITE— OR PAIRED WITH VIRTUALLY ANY OTHER COLOR—BLACK BECOMES AN ELEGANT ACCENT. THE OPPOSITE OF BLACK, WHITE HAS LONG BEEN A DECORATIVE FAVORITE. TODAY, IT IS USUALLY ASSOCIATED WITH THE MINIMALIST LOOK. THE MOST REFLECTIVE OF COLORS, WHITE HARMONIZES WITH ALL OTHER COLORS, WHETHER BRIGHT OR NEUTRAL. PAIRED WITH BLACK, IT PROVIDES A CLEAR, BOLD CONTRAST; PAIRED WITH GRAY, IT LENDS AN AIR OF TRANQUILITY AND SOPHISTICATION. GRAY CAN BE BLAND ON ITS OWN, BUT THE ADDITION OF DEEPER AND LIGHTER TONES WILL RESULT IN A BALANCED COLOR SCHEME. THE ADDITION OF METALLIC FITTINGS AND ACCESSORIES ENHANCES THE LOOK OF ALL THREE COLORS.

Gray *rag-rolling*

WHEN THE PAINT effects revolution ignited in the 1980s, rag-rolling was among the most widely used techniques. Its popularity remains, but a softer, more gentle approach is now favored. Today, the use of subtle, close color combinations lends an understated, contemporary twist to this finish.

There are two ways to apply the rag-rolling technique—the first uses the rag to roll the glaze on, and the second involves painting a glaze first, and then rag-rolling it off. Here we apply the first version of this technique. Rolling three tones of gray onto a white surface, we emulate the character and color of pale Carrara marble to create a cool, serene kitchen setting.

MATERIALS AND TOOLS
WHITE SATIN LATEX PAINT
IVORY HIGHLY PIGMENTED WOOD PAINT
SOFT BLACK HIGHLY PIGMENTED WOOD PAINT
HOUSEHOLD PAINTBRUSH
BADGER-HAIR SOFTENER
ARTISTS' SABLE BRUSH
VARNISH BRUSH
4 PAINT PAILS
LOW-TACK PAINTERS' TAPE
LARGE COTTON CLOTH
ACRYLIC GLAZING LIQUID
MATTE ACRYLIC VARNISH
SEMI-GLOSS ACRYLIC VARNISH (OPTIONAL)

1 • PREPARATION
This technique is best suited to solid wood and fiberboard doors—it is not appropriate for melamine, vinyl, or laminate doors. Prepare the surface following the instructions on pages 6-9. Apply two coats of white satin latex paint, allowing the first coat to dry thoroughly before applying the second.

2 • MIXING THE GLAZES
Create three colored glazes as follows: in three seperate paint pails, mix ivory and soft black wood paints to produce three tones of gray: pale, mid-tone, and darker. Add one-third acrylic glazing liquid and one-third equal amounts of matte acrylic varnish and water to each wood paint color.

3 • RAG-ROLLING THE FIRST GLAZE
Use low-tack painters' tape to mask off the door's outer panel. Cut a large cotton cloth into three pieces. Partially dip one piece of cloth into the mid-tone gray glaze, taking care not to saturate it. Work the glaze through the cloth, until the entire cloth has absorbed some of the glaze. Roll the cloth into a sausage shape, then lay it on the bottom left-hand corner of the door's inner panel. Using arcing movements, roll the cloth up the panel, repeating until the entire surface is evenly covered with ragging marks. Use a new rag when necessary.

4

5

4 • SOFTENING THE GLAZE

To soften and blend the effect of the rag-rolling, lightly dust a badger-hair softener over the still-wet glaze in all directions. Leave until thoroughly dry.

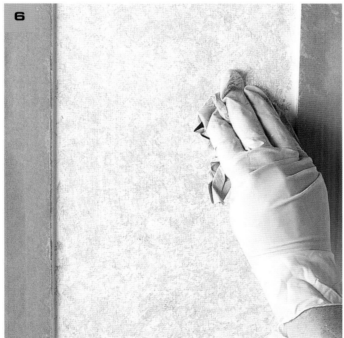

6

5 • RAG-ROLLING THE SECOND GLAZE

Remove the painters' tape from the outer panel and mask off the inner panel. Using a new rag, repeat the rag-rolling process on the outer panel, this time using the pale gray glaze. Once again, dust lightly with the softener, blending any hard edges or distinct marks. Leave for five minutes, then lightly rag on a touch of the mid-tone gray glaze. Blend once again with the softener, and allow to dry fully.

6 • RAG-ROLLING THE THIRD GLAZE

Remove the painters' tape from the inner panel, and mask off the outer panel once again. Using a new rag, take up the darker gray glaze and lightly roll it over the inner panel. Again, blend using the softener. Remove the tape from the outer panel, and check that the glaze has been evenly distributed over both the inner and outer panels; dab extra glaze onto any uneven patches. Soften once more, then allow to dry thoroughly.

7

7 • PAINTING IN DETAIL

Mask off the outer panel once again, so that the tape borders the inner panel. Mix a little ivory with some soft black wood paint in a paint pail to create a charcoal gray; add some water to thin out the paint. Using an artists' sable brush, paint the rim between the inner and outer panels. Paint an equally thin line along the very edge of the outer panel as well. Allow to dry thoroughly.

8 • FINISHING

Apply three coats of either matte or semi-gloss acrylic varnish, allowing each coat to dry thoroughly before applying the next. Do not use oil-based varnish, as this will yellow over time.

8

TRADE SECRETS

- *Do not overload the rag with glaze—if it is dripping or sodden, this means that it is oversaturated, and a new rag should be used for best effect.*

- *Always roll in arced lines rather than straight lines, so that the ragging marks are irregular. Rescrunching the cloth periodically will ensure that the same markings are not repeated.*

HARDWARE

Silver knobs or handles would subtly complement the various hues and tones of gray used here.

Vinegar glaze *fingerprinting*

THE TRADITION OF vinegar glazing began in the 19th century, when craftsmen used it as a cheap and simple solution to the increasing demand for graining on furniture and woodwork. Although not as sophisticated as some of the more formal glazes, vinegar glaze lends itself to numerous forms of pattern-making, such as printing with corks, putty, folded cards, and fingertips.

Here we work with a black glaze, making simple repetitive marks with the fingertip for a pewter chain-mail-like effect. The look is further embellished by a graphite varnish panel, and then finished with a high-gloss varnish for a stylish, contemporary feel.

1 • PREPARATION

This technique is only suitable for solid wood and fiberboard doors—it will not work on melamine, vinyl, or laminate surfaces. Prepare the surface following the instructions on pages 6-9. Apply two coats of ivory matte latex paint, letting the first coat dry before applying the second, and sanding between coats using fine-grade sandpaper. Sand again, then seal with a coat of white shellac brushed on as evenly as possible with a varnish brush.

2 • MIXING THE GLAZE

Put 8 tsp (40ml) of black powder pigment into a paint pail. Add a little malt vinegar, and mix into a paste. When the pigment has dissolved, add a cup (250ml) of vinegar (this will be enough for two doors), and mix thoroughly. Add three drops of black water-based universal tinter, 2 tsp (10ml) of dishwashing liquid or liquid soap, and 2 tsp (10ml) of white sugar. Stir until fully dissolved. The glaze should now be roughly the same consistency as skimmed milk.

MATERIALS AND TOOLS

IVORY MATTE LATEX PAINT
BLACK POWDER PIGMENT
BLACK WATER-BASED UNIVERSAL TINTER
HOUSEHOLD PAINTBRUSH
4 VARNISH BRUSHES
MALT VINEGAR
DISHWASHING LIQUID OR LIQUID SOAP
WHITE SUGAR
PAINT PAIL
LOW-TACK PAINTERS' TAPE
FINE-GRADE SANDPAPER
WHITE SHELLAC
READY-MADE WATER-BASED GRAPHITE VARNISH OR
METALLIC VARNISH TINTED WITH BLACK
UNIVERSAL TINTER
GLOSS ACRYLIC VARNISH

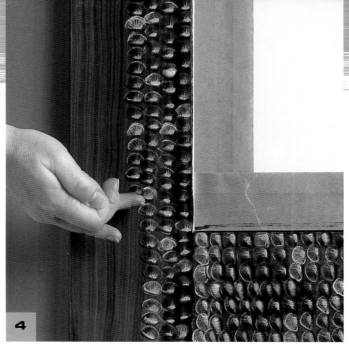

4 • FINGERPRINTING

Before you start fingerprinting, you may wish to experiment with the different marks made by the different points of your fingertip, and with applying different amounts of pressure. When you are ready to start fingerprinting, press the side of your third fingertip firmly down on the wet glaze, and start to print in rows, working from the inside to the outside of the border. Because each print will be slightly different, the pattern will be somewhat uneven, but this is part of the charm of this technique.

3 • APPLYING THE GLAZE

Use low-tack painters' tape to mask off the inner panel of the door. Using a varnish brush, apply a generous, even coat of glaze to the outer panel. Brush the coat through several times to ensure even coverage. The glaze will naturally bubble as it is applied; you'll need to brush out the larger bubbles, but the smaller ones should disappear on their own.

5 • GLAZING THE INNER PANEL

Add three or four more drops of black universal tinter to the glaze. Remove the tape from the inner panel, then carefully paint with the darkened glaze. Allow to dry thoroughly.

6

HARDWARE
Silver or pewter handles or knobs echo the metallic look of this cool, modern finish.

TRADE SECRETS

- *Because the ingredients of this glaze are only lightly bound together, it must always be sealed with shellac.*

- *Work in a ventilated space, as the vinegar smell can become pungent and overpowering.*

6 • SEALING
Glide a coat of white shellac onto the outer panel, leaving the inner panel clear. Allow to dry thoroughly.

7

7 • VARNISHING
Lay on a coat of ready-made water-based graphite varnish or metallic varnish tinted with black universal tinter in smooth horizontal strokes, then lay it off in vertical strokes of the same direction (finish with all strokes brushing either upward or downward, but not both). Allow to dry, then apply a second coat in the same way. Leave until completely dry.

8 • FINISHING
Apply three even coats of gloss acrylic varnish to the entire door for a high-sheen finish, allowing each coat to dry thoroughly before applying the next.

Silver squares *on white*

LIGHTER AND LESS PRONOUNCED than gold, silver lends itself to minimalist fashions, especially when used together with white, ivory, and pale gray. Here we introduce a quick, simple gilding technique using aluminum metal leaf—a cheaper but effective alternative to real silver leaf—on ivory with a high-gloss finish, to add a crisp and chic lift to plain painted doors. The essence of simplicity, this finish will bring an easygoing, modern style to your kitchen. Accessorize with plenty of chrome and silver details to emphasize the contemporary feel.

1 • PREPARATION
Prepare a solid wood, fiberboard, vinyl, melamine or laminate surface following the instructions on pages 6-9. Apply two coats of ivory matte latex paint or wood paint, letting the first coat dry before applying the second. Sand between coats using fine-grade sandpaper on a wooden door only. When fully dry, sand until smooth.

2 • CUTTING THE SQUARES
Using a pencil and ruler, draw 3 in (75mm) squares onto the backing paper of the aluminum leaf transfer. Cut them out with sharp dressmaking scissors or a craft knife, using a metal ruler to ensure straight lines. You will need five squares per door.

MATERIALS AND TOOLS
IVORY MATTE LATEX PAINT OR HIGHLY PIGMENTED WOOD PAINT
HOUSEHOLD PAINTBRUSH
VARNISH BRUSH
FITCH BRUSH
½ IN (13MM) ONE-STROKE BRUSH
ALUMINUM METAL LEAF TRANSFER
METAL RULER
PENCIL
SHARP DRESSMAKING SCISSORS OR CRAFT KNIFE
ACRYLIC GILDING SIZE
FINE-GRADE SANDPAPER
WHITE SHELLAC
GLOSS ACRYLIC VARNISH

3 • MARKING UP
This design is essentially random, so the squares should be placed irregularly. Lay the squares out onto the door until you have achieved the right balance. Using a pencil and ruler, lightly draw the squares in position onto the door. Draw each square a little smaller than the transfer leaf, so that the pencil marks will be completely covered by the aluminum square.

4 • SEALING THE SQUARES

Take up a little white shellac on a fitch brush and carefully brush it inside each drawn square. Go slightly over the lines to accommodate those aluminum squares that are a bit larger than the pencil squares. Leave until completely dry.

5 • SIZING THE SQUARES

Using a $\frac{1}{2}$ in (13mm) one-stroke brush, paint acrylic gilding size onto each square, covering exactly the area of the shellac. Leave for about 15 minutes, or until the size is translucent.

6 • APPLYING THE ALUMINUM LEAF

Position an aluminum square over a sized square, making sure it is lined up, then lay it down carefully. Smooth over the transfer paper backing with your fingertips. Stick each square down in the same way, then smooth each one down one final time before carefully peeling off the transfer backing paper.

7

TRADE SECRETS

- *Think about how your cupboard doors relate to each other when designing the layout of squares for each door. To practice, make some paper squares and stick them on the doors, moving them around until you like the design. The more cupboards you have, the fewer squares you will need.*

- *If your cupboards close flush, think about running a single square across two doors—to do this, just cut the square in half.*

- *Aluminum leaf works best with gloss acrylic varnish; oil-based varnish can dull its shine or cause it to yellow, making the metal appear tarnished.*

7 • SEALING
Paint over each square with white shellac to seal and protect the gilded areas. Allow to dry completely.

8 • FINISHING
Use a varnish brush to apply three thin, even coats of gloss acrylic varnish, allowing each coat to dry thoroughly before applying the next.

8

HARDWARE
Chrome or silver handles or knobs will complete the look of this stylish, cool, contemporary design.

Modern classics

Usually associated with a modern look, black, white, and gray are actually suited to a diverse range of decorative styles. A wide variety of design possibilities is shown here, including a pewter-like liming finish, an elegant Japanese-style hand-painted design, a pastel gray combed finish, and a sparkling spattered and distressed effect in gray and silver.

▼ LIMING ON BLACK

Apply liming paste over black for a pewter-like effect. Brush on a coat of black wood paint. When dry, apply liming paste (see Step 5, page 81). When dry, rub it away using a small, soft wire brush, working in the direction of the grain (see Step 6, page 82). Seal with white shellac. When dry, apply three coats of matte acrylic varnish. *Suitable for open-grained hardwoods.*

▲ JAPANESE-STYLE ORCHID DESIGN

This simple, delicate design creates a light, clean look. After priming, apply two coats of ivory matte latex or wood paint. Draw an orchid shape (taken from a flower book) onto tracing paper in pencil and transfer onto the inner panel. Tint matte acrylic varnish gray and brush onto the panel, then stipple (see Liquid glaze effects, page 19). Mark up two vertical and five horizontal lines. Stick down a double row of low-tack lining tape on the horizontal lines. Paint between the taped lines using gray artists' acrylic paint, avoiding the orchid design. Remove the tapes when dry and tape up and paint between the vertical lines. When dry, paint in the orchid using white and ivory acrylic paints; use pale gray for highlights, shadows, and leaves. Paint the outer panel with ivory matte latex paint tinted gray. Apply three coats of matte acrylic varnish. *Suitable for all surfaces.*

▼ COOL GRAY COMBING

Cool pastel gray stripes create a stylish, refined look. After priming (see pages 6–9), apply a coat of pastel gray matte latex or wood paint. Mask off the outer panel. Tint some combing paste to a mid-tone gray using black tinter (see Step 2, page 52). Brush a thick, even layer onto the inner panel and comb through with a rubber comb (see Steps 3 and 4, page 53). After 24 hours, remove the tape. Touch up any uneven sections with the pastel gray paint. Use medium-grade steel wool to burnish the outer frame. Apply three coats of semi-gloss acrylic varnish to the frame and three coats of matte acrylic varnish to the inner panel.

Suitable for wooden and fiberboard surfaces.

▲ OFF-WHITE WITH BLACK CRAQUELURE

Craquelure varnish is used here for a simple, classic style. After priming (see pages 6–9), apply two coats of off-white matte latex or wood paint. Mask off the outer panel and apply both steps of craquelure varnish to the inner panel. After a few hours, rub Payne's gray artists' oil paint into the cracks (see Step 4, page 61); remove excess oil paint with a lint-free cloth. After 24 hours, seal with white shellac. When dry, apply semi-gloss acrylic varnish. Remove the tape. Paint the rim around the inside panel with charcoal gray stencil paint. If the door is wooden, lightly sand the outer panel to reveal some of the wood grain. Seal with matte acrylic varnish.

Suitable for wooden and fiberboard surfaces.

▼ **HAND-PAINTED RELIEF STENCILING**

This stenciled duck design is ideal for a waterfront home. The door does not need priming. Apply a coat of pale gray matte latex or wood paint. When dry, rub back with coarse-grade sandpaper to reveal the wood beneath. Stencil ducks onto the inner panel with impasto or thick-textured paint (see Step 3, page 31). Dilute pale gray and blue-gray wood paint and paint over the dry stencil motif, painting the eyes with charcoal gray. Apply a gray wash to the molding. When dry, use fine-grade sandpaper to gently rub the stenciling to reveal the impasto or thick-textured paint (see Step 8, page 32). Apply white wax (see Colored wax, page 23) and buff 10 minutes later, or, near sink areas, apply matte acrylic varnish tinted white.
Suitable for wooden surfaces.

▲ **SILVER SPATTER AND DISTRESSED GILDING**

Aluminum leaf and gray and silver spatter combine to produce a dazzling style. After priming (see pages 6–9), apply one coat of pale gray matte latex or wood paint. Add a drop of black and raw umber universal tinters to some of the paint and dab onto the door with a sea sponge. Mask off the molding. Mix up a mid-tone gray glaze to the consistency of milk using ⅔ matte acrylic varnish, ⅓ water, and black and white tinters. Spatter the door (see Liquid glaze effects, page 19). Darken the glaze with a little black and spatter again. Darken again and spatter once more. Dilute the original gray paint and spatter. Finally, spatter with diluted silver paint. Allow to dry overnight, then remove the tape. Glide white shellac onto the molding; when dry, gild with aluminum transfer metal leaf (see Steps 5-6, page 117). Dip medium-grade steel wool in white shellac and rub on the gilded areas to distress the metal leaf. When dry, apply three coats of semi-gloss acrylic varnish.
Suitable for wooden and fiberboard surfaces.

▼ **SILVER CRACKLE GLAZE**

A modern metallic-style effect. After priming (see pages 6–9), apply two coats of pale gray matte latex or wood paint. Mask off the outer panel and glide white shellac onto the inner panel. Gild aluminum transfer metal leaf to cover the whole inner panel (see Step 6, page 117) and seal with white shellac. When dry, vertically brush on a coat of crackle glaze. Brush the pale gray paint horizontally over the dry crackle glaze; do not brush over the same area twice. Once dry, seal with matte polyurethane varnish (see Polyurethane varnish, page 23) and allow to dry overnight. Remove the tape, then paint the outer panel a very matte pale gray. When dry, apply three coats of metallic varnish (see Metallic varnishes, page 23).
Suitable for all surfaces.

▲ **SILVER STENCILING ON BLACK**

Stencil silver highlights over glossy black for an art-deco style. Apply a coat of primer tinted black (see pages 6–9), followed by two coats of black matte latex or wood paint. Seal with white shellac. Select a linear stencil, spray low-tack adhesive on its back, and lay it centrally on the outside panel. Stencil with silver stencil or wood paint. Repeat the process up the lengths of each vertical panel. Hand-paint a silver line around the inner rim of the panel. When dry, apply three coats of gloss acrylic varnish.
Suitable for all surfaces.

Resource directory

Many of the tools and materials used in this book can be found at hardware and fine art stores. Check the Yellow Pages for the location nearest you. Otherwise, you can order by mail or online from any of the following suppliers:

ABSOLUTE COATINGS INC.
38 Portman Road
New Rochelle, NY 10081
Tel (914) 636-0700
Fax (914) 636-0822
Web www.lastnlast.com
Varnishes and sealers. Information package available.

ADELE BISHOP
5575 N Services Road
Burlington, ON L7L 6M1
Tel (905) 319-0051
Fax (905) 319-0676
Web www.adelebishop.com
Pre-cut stencils and art supplies.

ALBERT CONSTANTINE & SONS
2050 Eastchester Road
Bronx, NY 10461
Toll-Free 1-800-223-8087
Outside U.S. (718) 792-2110
Toll-Free Fax 1-800-253-9663
Web www.constantines.com
Specialist decorating materials, crackle varnish, stencils, oil glaze. Also in Florida.

ART ESSENTIAL OF NEW YORK LTD.
3 Cross Street
Suffern, NY 10901-4601
Toll-Free 1-800-283-5323
Gold leaf and gilding tools.

ARTISAN SUPPLY CO.
5910 Arsenal
St. Louis, MO 63139
Tel (314) 645-4795
Email fauxtools@aol.com
Web www.members.aol.com/fauxtools
Decorative painting tools, including stipplers, badger-hair softeners, blenders, floggers, gilding brushes and plaster blades.

BAYSIDE PAINT COMPANY
3603 Camino Del Rio West
San Diego, CA 92110
Tel (619) 487-6006
Fax (619) 688-0082
Web www.baysidepaintcompany.com
Variety of quality paints, brushes and faux finishing products.

BEST LIEBCO CORPORATION
1201 Jackson Street
Philadelphia, PA 19148
Toll-Free 1-800-523-9095
Fax (215) 463-0988
Email bestliebco@aol.com
Specialty brushes for paint effects, including mottlers, softeners, stipplers, sponges, floggers, blenders, and splatter brushes. Contact for local retailers.

BLUE RIBBON STENCILS
26 S Horton Street
Dayton, OH 45403
Tel (937) 254-2319
Web www.blueribbonstencils.com
Over 90 pre-cut stencil designs. Online retailer directory.

BRIWAX WOODCARE PRODUCTS
220 South Main Street
Auburn, ME 04210
Toll-Free 1-800-274-9299
24-hr Fax Line (212) 504 9550
Web www.BriwaxWoodcare.com
Shellacs, varnishes and wood waxes.

THE CHESHIRE CAT
538 3rd Street
Canmore, AB T1W 2J4
Tel (403) 678-3212
Web www.cheshirecatstencils.com
Pre-cut stencil distributor. Wide variety.

CONSTANTINE'S
2050 Eastchester Road
Bronx, NY 10461
Toll-Free 1-800-223-8087
Fax (718) 792-2110
Metallic varnishes, gilding creams and waxes, white shellac, button polish shellac, gold leaf products.

DESIGNER STENCILS
c/o The Designer Shoppe, Inc.
3634 Silverside Road
Wilmington, DL 19810
Toll-Free 1-800-822-7836
Tel (302) 475-5663
Fax (302) 477-0170
Web www.designerstencils.com
Over 1100 pre-cut stencil designs, including lettering, plus supplies.

DOVER PUBLICATIONS
11 East Ninth Avenue
New York, NY 10019
Tel (212) 255-6399
Reference books, period paints, ready-to-cut stencil designs.

DRESSLER STENCIL COMPANY
253 SW 41st Street
Renton, WA 98055
Toll-Free 1-888-656-4515
Fax (425) 656-4381
Web www.dresslerstencils.com
Over 300 pre-cut stencil designs.

FINE PAINTS OF EUROPE
PO Box 419, Route 4 West
Woodstock, VT 05091
Toll-Free 1-800-332-1556
Fax (802) 457-1740
Web www.fine-paints.com
Importer of Schreuder high-pigment paints. Online retail directory.

FIRENZE ENTERPRISES, INC.
12976 SW 132 Avenue
Miami, FL 33186
Tel (305) 232-0233
Fax (305) 232-3191
Web www.rivesto-marmorino.com
Distributor of marmorino in 27 premixed colors, plus Italian-made trowels.

FROG TOOL COMPANY LTD.
2169 IL Route 26
Dixon, IL 61021
Tel (815) 288-3811
Fax (815) 288-3919
Paint strippers, brushes, varnishes.

FULLER-O'BRIEN CORP
450 East Grand Avenue
South San Francisco, CA 84033
Toll-Free 1-888-681-6353 #2
Web www.fullerpaint.com
Paints. Online dealer locator.

GOLDEN ARTIST COLORS, INC.
188 Bell Road
New Berlin, NY 13411-9527
Toll-Free 1-888-397-2468
Fax (607) 847-6767
Web www.goldenpaints.com
Artists' acrylic paints, retardants, mediums, and varnishes. Online dealer locator.

HOMESTEAD HOUSE AUTHENTIC MILK PAINT
95 Niagara Street
Toronto, ON M5V 1C3
Tel (416) 504-9984
Distributor of milk paint products. Call for color chart and retailer locations.

JANOVIC
771 Ninth Avenue
New York, NY 10019
Tel (212) 245-3241
Web www.janovic.com
Paints and specialist brushes.

KREMER PIGMENTS INC.
228 Elizabeth Street
New York, NY 10012
Toll-Free 1-800-995-5501
Fax (212) 219-2394
Web www.kremer-pigmente.de
Cadmium, natural earth, pearl luster, and iron oxide pigments; metal powders, powdered stains, organic dyes.

L.A. STENCILWORKS
16115 Vanowen Street
Van Nuys, CA 91406
Toll-Free 1-877-989-0262
Tel (818) 989-0262
Fax (818) 989-0405
Web www.lastencilwork.com
Pre-cut themed stencils, including designs from Morocco, Italy, Mexico, and Asia, plus supplies.

LEE VALLEY TOOLS LTD.
PO Box 6295, Station J
Ottawa, ON Canada K2A 1TA
Toll-Free 1-800-267-8767
Toll-Free Fax 1-800-668-1807
OR
P.O. Box 1780
Ogdensburg, NY 13669-6780
Toll-Free 1-800-871-8158
Toll-Free Fax 1-800-513-7885
Web www.leevalley.com
Shellac flake in white (clear), orange (amber), garnet (deep red) and other finishes. Mail-order and Canadian locations.

LIBERON/STAR WOOD FINISH
SUPPLY
PO Box 86
Mendocino, CA 95460
Toll-Free 1-800-245-5611
Fax (707) 962-9484
Web www.woodfinishsupply.com
Wood-finishing materials, paints and varnishes. Online dealer locator.

THE MAD STENCILIST
PO Box 5497 Dept N
El Dorado Hills, CA 95762
Toll-Free 1-888-882-6232
Fax (916) 933-7873
Web www.madstencilist.com
Over 170 pre-cut stencil designs.

MOHAWK FINISHING PRODUCTS
INC.
Route 30 North
Amsterdam, NY 12010
Tel (518) 843-1380
Crackle varnish, polishes, shellacs. Atlanta, Dallas, California locations.

THE OLD FASHIONED MILK PAINT
CO.
436 Main Street
PO Box 222
Groton, MA 01450
Tel (978) 448-6336
Fax (978) 448-2754
Canada (416) 364-1393
Web www.milkpaint.com
Powdered milk paint in a wide range of colors. Online dealer locator.

PAINT AND DECORATING
RETAILERS ASSOCIATION
403 Axminister Drive
St. Louis, MO 63026-2941
Tel (636) 326-2636
Fax (636) 326-1823
Web www.pdra.org
U.S./Canada trade association. Online directory of paint and decorative supply retailers.

PAINT EFFECTS
2426 Fillmore Street
San Francisco, CA 94115
Tel (415) 292-7780
Fax (415) 292-7782
Web www.painteffects.com
Decorative paint, decoupage, and stenciling supplies, including colored glazing liquid, craquelure, decoupage lacquer, varnishing and antiquing waxes, liming paste, and brushes, tools, and stencils.

PAINT MAGIC
412 Pebble Creek Court
Pennington, NJ 08534
Toll-Free 1-877-330-0445
Fax (609) 737-7333
Email PntMgc@aol.com
Web www.desmondint.com/
PaintMagic
Prepared paint solutions including colorwash, emulsions, glazing liquid, craquelure, patina, impasto, limewash, marmorino, primers, distemper, and suede paint. Canadian orders call for details.

PEARL PAINTS
308 Canal Street
New York, NY 10013
Toll-Free 1-800-221-6845 x2297
Web www.pearlpaint.com
Paints and fine art supplies, including metallic varnishes, gilding creams and waxes, white shellac, button polish shellac, gold leaf products, textured gels, and dry pigments. Online retail location directory.

PERIWINKLE ESSENTIAL STENCILS
PO Box 457
West Kennebunk, ME 04094
Tel (207) 985-8020
Fax (207) 985-1601
Web www.cybertours.com/
periwinkle
Pre-cut stencil patterns, including botanical paintings, Delft pottery patterns, and William Morris designs.

PIERRE FINKELSTEIN INSTITUTE OF
DECORATIVE PAINTING, INC.
20 West 20th Street, Suite 1009
New York, NY 10011
Toll-Free 1-888-328-9278
Web www.pfinkelstein.com
European specialty brushes by mail order. Online catalog and order form.

PORTER'S ORIGINAL PAINTS
Sydney, Australia
Tel (818) 623-9394
Fax (818) 623-9210
Web www.porters.com.au
Limewash, French wash, milk paint, wood paint, distemper, fresco, liquid copper and patina green, liquid iron and instant rust, Roman cement. U.S. office ships to Canada.

PRATT & LAMBERT INC.
PO Box 22
Buffalo, NY 14240
Web www.prattandlambert.com
Paints, ready-mixed glazes and varnishes. Online store locator; in Canada call 1-800-289-7728.

R&F HANDMADE PAINTS, INC.
110 Prince Street
Kingston, NY 12401
Toll-Free 1-800-206-8088
Fax (914) 331-3242
Web www.rfpaints.com
Hand-made paints, pigment sticks and encaustics. Online retailer directory.

RENOVATOR'S SUPPLY INC.
Renovator's Old Mill
Millers Falls, MA 10349
Tel (413) 659-3773
General art supplies.

SEPP LEAF PRODUCTS, INC.
381 Park Avenue South
New York, NY 10016
Toll-Free 1-800-971-7377
Tel (212) 683-2840
Fax (212) 725-0308
Email sales@seppleaf.com
Web www.seppleaf.com
Gold and metal leaf, plus supplies and tools. Gilding creams and waxes, wood finishing and restoration products. Kolcaustico Venetian plaster. Metallic varnishes, white shellac, and button polish shellac.

THE SIMS COLLECTION
24 Tower Crescent
Barrie, ON L4N 2V2
Tel (705) 725-0152
Fax (705) 725-8637
Web www.simsdesigns.com
Pre-cut stencils in whimsical designs.

SINOPIA LLC
229 Valencia Street
San Francisco, CA 94103
Tel (415) 621-2898
Fax (415) 621 2897
Web www.sinopia.com
Kremer pigments, metal powders and filings, mica flakes, bronzing powders, colored marble dust, Venetian plaster, gilding materials, specialty brushes, shellacs, waxes, varnishes, acrylic glazing liquids. Online catalogue.

STENCIL HOUSE OF NEW
HAMPSHIRE
PO Box 16109
Hooksett, NH 03106
Toll-Free 1-800-622-9416
Tel (603) 625-1716
Web www.stencilhouse.com
Over 230 primarily floral pre-cut stencils, plus supplies.

STENCILS BY NANCY
15219 Stuebner Airline, Suite 5
Houston, TX 77069
Tel (281) 893-2227
Fax (281) 893-6733
Web www.stencilsbynancy.net
Whimsical pre-cut stencils.

THE TEXSTON COMPANY
8011 Webb Avenue
North Hollywood, CA 91605
Toll-Free 1-800-788-7113
Tel (818) 768-7676
Fax (818) 768-6773
Web www.texston.com
Veneciano, marmorino and terra plaster products, available untinted or tinted.

WOODCRAFTER'S SUPPLY CORP.
5331 Sinclair Road
Columbus, OH 43229
Toll-free 1-800-225-1153
Web www.woodcraft.com
Paint strippers and varnishes.

Index

Credits

The author and Quarto would like to thank Paint Magic Ltd for all of the wonderful paint supplies, and PWS Distributors Ltd for contributing the cupboard doors. We are also grateful to the following door hardware companies for lending knobs and handles for photography: House of Brass (UK 44 115 947 5430), Locks & Handles, Architectural Components Ltd (UK 44 10 7581 2401), and PWS Distributors Ltd (UK 44 1325 50 55 55).

Author acknowledgements
My thanks to Steffanie Diamond Brown and Sally Bond, and to the rest of the Quarto team, who worked with complete enthusiasm, drive and commitment throughout the project. Thanks also to Paul Forrester for many, many patient hours behind the camera, and to Katharyn Quinn and Zoe Miller for their help in priming and organizing the painted cupboard doors.

Collage extracts from Mrs. Beeton's Book of Household Management have been reproduced by kind permission of Wardlock Publishing. Decoupage motifs and stencils have been reproduced by kind permission of The Stencil Library.

Quarto would like to acknowledge and thank the following for supplying pictures reproduced in this book:

(key: l left, r right, c center, t top, b bottom)

p26tr Mark Wilkinson Furniture Limited, bl The Artisan Kitchen and Furniture by John Lewis of Hungerford, p27br Roundhouse Design, p42 Paula Rosa, p43br Mark Wilkinson Furniture Limited, p46 Scottwood of Nottingham, p47b Simon Taylor Furniture, p70 Chalon UK Limited, p71tr Creative Decorating, p88 Mark Wilkinson Furniture Limited, p89br Mark Wilkinson Furniture Limited, p106 Mark Wilkinson Furniture Limited, p107bl Regency Kitchens

All other photographs and illustrations are the copyright of Quarto.
While every effort has been made to credit contributors, Quarto would like to apologize should there have been any omissions or errors.

For Liberty

Text and illustration copyright © 1994 Nicola Smee
First published by ORCHARD BOOKS, 96 Leonard Street,
London EC2A 4RH.
Published in the United States by BridgeWater Books, an imprint of
Troll Associates.

Library of Congress Cataloging-in-Publication Data

Smee, Nicola.
The Tusk Fairy / Nicola Smee.
p.   cm.
Summary: When Lizzie's well-worn knitted elephant unravels to
nothing, leaving only the tusks, Grandma suggests leaving the
remains for the Tooth Fairy to see what will happen.
ISBN 0-8167-3311-2 (lib. bdg.)   ISBN 0-8167-3312-0 (pbk.)
[1. Toys—Fiction. 2. Elephants—Fiction. 3. Grandmothers—
Fiction. 4. Tooth Fairy—Fiction.] I. Title.
PZ7.S6396Tu   1994
[E]—dc20   93-28444
Printed in Belgium

10 9 8 7 6 5 4 3 2 1

The Tusk Fairy

Nicola Smee

BridgeWater Books

Lizzie's favorite toy was her knitted Elephant.

Grandma had given him to Lizzie on the day she was born, so they were exactly the same age.

They had been through a lot together. . .

and over the years Elephant began to look the worse for wear.

When Elephant's trunk started to unravel,
Lizzie bandaged it with some ribbon.

When his feet started to wear out and
stuffing poked through his knees,

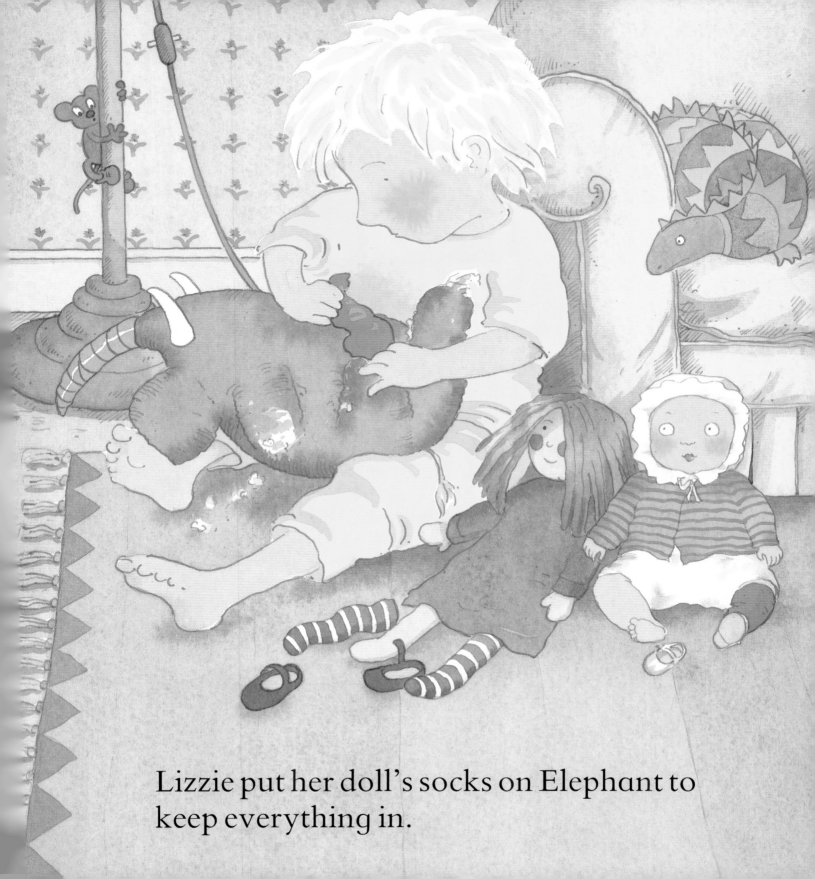

Lizzie put her doll's socks on Elephant to keep everything in.

Then, when the wool on Elephant's back got so thin you could see his insides, Lizzie removed Teddy's pants.

She put them on Elephant to keep him together.

Then one day a TERRIBLE thing happened!

Lizzie was giving her toys a ride when a thread from Elephant's ear got caught on a thorn.

By the time she noticed, all that was left of Elephant was two tusks!

Lizzie followed the trail back, picking up the pants, the socks, bits of stuffing, the ribbon, and the unraveled wool.

Then she sat down and cried and cried and cried.
Grandma ran out to see what had happened.

"Why don't you put the tusks under your pillow for the Tooth Fairy?" she said.

So that night, Lizzie put the tusks under
her pillow and tried to sleep, while
Grandma hunted for some gray wool.

Lizzie fell into a deep dreamy sleep, so she didn't hear Grandma's knitting needles clicking through the night.

The next morning, Grandma was
awakened by Lizzie's cries of delight.
"THE TUSK FAIRY'S BEEN HERE!
THE TUSK FAIRY'S BEEN HERE!"

Grandma was tired but also very happy.
She had been worried when she found
she had run out of gray wool—but it
didn't seem to bother Lizzie.

And fond as they had been of Old Elephant, the toys were pleased to see New Elephant, because it meant they got their clothes back.